Overcoming Obstacles

The Journey of
Project WeHOPE

Alicia Garcia

authorHOUSE®

AuthorHouse™
1663 Liberty Drive
Bloomington, IN 47403
www.authorhouse.com
Phone: 1 (800) 839-8640

Published by AuthorHouse 09/29/2017

ISBN: 978-1-5462-1077-1 (sc)
ISBN: 978-1-5462-1078-8 (hc)
ISBN: 978-1-5462-1079-5 (e)

Library of Congress Control Number: 2017914910

Print information available on the last page.

Contents

Contents

Acknowledgements

I WOULD LIKE TO THANK MY parents for raising me to believe in myself and providing me with morals and values to recognize the importance of education, collaboration and family. Thank you dad for being such a positive role model. I would also like to thank my sister Angel Wolf for being the first person to read through my edited manuscript. You inspire me! And to my beautiful sister Anita Blount, thank you for your love and support. You are amazing and "it's in the wash!"

I would like to thank Patten University for showing me that the only obstacles there are in my life are the ones that I place upon myself. I would like to thank Pastor Yaahn Hunter for encouraging me to write this book, supporting me and believing in me. I would like to give a very special thank you to Dr. Karen Ensor and Dr. Kathy Fairbanks for editing this book. You have always supported and encouraged me. You help me to grow in ways that I never imagined possible.

Thank you Pastor Timothy Russell and the Renaissance Entrepreneurship Center team for your kindness and for all of the hard work you do in the community. You literally help people change their lives.

Thank you Pastor Paul and Evangelist Cheryl Bains for giving tirelessly, loving endlessly, and providing me with overwhelming support. I stand in awe at the amazing things you have done. I am blessed to be part of your team.

A special thanks to my family, friends, Saint Samuel Church

members, students, and Project WeHOPE employees. You have all played a vital role in who I am and where I am today. I love you all. Thank you for your support.

Last but certainly not least, I would like to thank my very handsome husband Joshua. Thank you for being my #1 fan. Thank you for believing in me and showing me unconditional love. I dedicate this book to you.

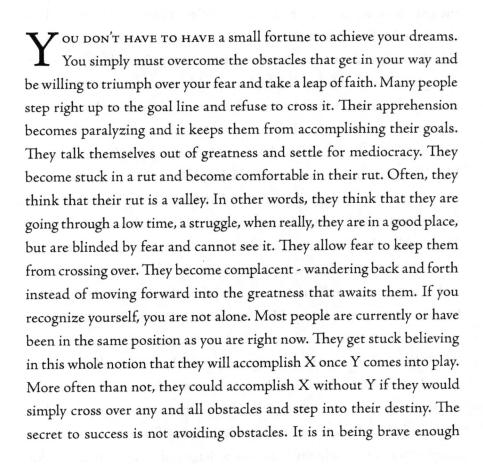

Chapter 1

A Little History

Y OU DON'T HAVE TO HAVE a small fortune to achieve your dreams. You simply must overcome the obstacles that get in your way and be willing to triumph over your fear and take a leap of faith. Many people step right up to the goal line and refuse to cross it. Their apprehension becomes paralyzing and it keeps them from accomplishing their goals. They talk themselves out of greatness and settle for mediocracy. They become stuck in a rut and become comfortable in their rut. Often, they think that their rut is a valley. In other words, they think that they are going through a low time, a struggle, when really, they are in a good place, but are blinded by fear and cannot see it. They allow fear to keep them from crossing over. They become complacent - wandering back and forth instead of moving forward into the greatness that awaits them. If you recognize yourself, you are not alone. Most people are currently or have been in the same position as you are right now. They get stuck believing in this whole notion that they will accomplish X once Y comes into play. More often than not, they could accomplish X without Y if they would simply cross over any and all obstacles and step into their destiny. The secret to success is not avoiding obstacles. It is in being brave enough to overcome them. Take a risk! There you will find joy, fulfillment, and greatness.

'Faith is taking the first step, even when you don't see the whole staircase (Martin Luther King Jr).'

This profound statement by Martin Luther King Jr outlines the life and ministry of Pastor Paul Bains and his journey to becoming an entrepreneur, marrying the love of his life, pastoring Saint Samuel Church of God in Christ, and starting a non-profit organization that would touch tens of thousands of lives. His upbringing led him to have an enormous vision. His faith in God gave him the courage to pursue the grandiose ideas in his heart with reckless abandon. He learned to overcome his fear and do whatever was necessary to achieve greatness. Yes, there were many obstacles that got in his way. Several of them were very painful and came with a high price. However, he has a stubborn tenacity that drives him. His creative and tactical thinking have helped him endure the worst of times.

Paul Jeremiah Bains was born in December of 1961 to William Lloyd Bains (commonly known as W.L.) and Mary Celeste Crittle Bains. His parents were devout Christians and members of the Church of God in Christ, the world's largest predominately African American Church. They lived in San Francisco, California, but eventually relocated to Palo Alto, California. W.L. was a painter by trade. He was a perfectionist and made a point to do his best at everything he did. While painting, his work was extraordinary. He was not one to settle for being a good painter; he was determined to be the best. He grew up in a time when racial discrimination was running rampant. He did not allow that to deter him. It was a big obstacle to overcome. He recognized he had to prove himself in ways in which other people were not required. He embraced this obstacle and took pride in being Black. It wasn't in an arrogant way. He simply embraced his heritage and was not afraid to take a risk. He recognized that Blacks have a different struggle than other races so he instilled in his children the importance of a good education, strong work ethic, and solid plans for their futures. After all, he wanted his children to strive for their best.

W.L. grew up in Texas, so he was not a stranger to etiquette and hospitality. He had numerous principles and values which guided his decisions and impacted his family. He was not one to allow circumstances to deter him. He was going to find a way to get around all hindrances. If he couldn't get around them, he would climb over them or simply move them out of the way. It was this determination which lead him to pursue his dreams and develop a strong work ethic. He lived by the scripture found in Colossians 3:23-24 (NIV)

'And whatsoever ye do, do it heartily, as to the Lord, and not unto men; Knowing that of the Lord ye shall receive the reward of the inheritance: for ye serve the Lord Christ.'

He believed that doing your best was not an act of greatness or nobility; it was a general expectation, especially if you considered yourself to be a child of God.

Another trait that must be noted about W.L. Bains is that he was very innovative for his day. He was well known for his entrepreneurial mind and the way in which he could communicate Scripture to his congregation. He was an excellent orator and a well-respected member of the community. People still refer to his sermons as having been enlightening, inspiring, and messages that they had never heard before. He was not afraid to take a risk or follow his principles, even if it went against whatever was popular. One example of this is how he allowed women to speak from the pulpit at a time where that was completely unheard of. He was a renaissance man. He did not believe in living on the edge of greatness. He was determined to experience greatness to its fullest extent. Due to his intellect, some of the locals referred to him as 'Dr. Bains.' He was extremely diversified, having a wealth of knowledge in various industries. He had a radio broadcast in San Francisco and was in *Jet*, a still popular national magazine for African American's featuring success stories in the African American community. He was featured in this magazine because of his benevolent service and accomplishments in the African American community.

His passion and determination caused him to project grand expectations on those who served under his leadership. He believed that everyone should give their best, especially in the house of God. He felt strongly that, 'God is not interested in your left overs. He wants your first fruit. Give God your best.' Due to this stringent belief, he would 'call people on the carpet' when they didn't do their best. For some, this motivated them to rise to the occasion and grow. Others could not handle his expectations and viewed him as an arduous task master. Nevertheless, no matter how they perceived him, they respected him.

Prior to founding Saint Samuel Church of God in Christ, named after his deceased son, W.L. served in the Army. During his tenure in the service, he was a boxer. His wife Mary worked at Stanford in the kitchen and eventually became a Stanford nurse for over 30 years. She was a great cook and loving wife. They had eight children, four girls and four boys. They were a close-knit family. All the children were taught to value one another and to be obedient to God as well as their parents. Their traditional church positioned them to be different than the children in which they were surrounded. For example, one of their church denominational teachings did not permit girls to wear pants. This did not allow for any exception. Consequently, the girls were not permitted to dress out for P.E. This required speaking to teachers and the principal. W.L. understood the rules of the school, but he stated, 'The rules of God supersede the rules of any institution.'

This belief was based on the Scripture found in Deuteronomy 22:5 (NIV) which states, 'A woman shall not wear anything that pertains to a man, nor shall a man put on a woman's garment, for all who do so are an abomination to the Lord your God.' They stood by their principles and beliefs despite the protests of the teachers and the protests of some of their children.

Another strict adherence to biblical principles that they followed was being hospitable to one another. They believed in feeding the hungry and providing a place to stay if they could do so. Because of this belief, the children would often come home from school and find evangelists or other young people without a place to stay were now living with them temporarily. This practice birthed hospitality in all the children which continues to exist in their adulthood. Many of them still have different friends, extended family members, or simply people in need living in their homes at this very moment. They were by no means financially wealthy, however they passed on a lot of wealth to their children by other means. Being their 'brother's keeper' is one aspect of the legacy that W.L and Mary left to their children, who have gone on to help numerous people in need and to encourage them to pursue excellence and persevere.

Additionally, W.L. was a generous man. He owned a parking lot in San Francisco on Broadway for several years. Instead of selling it for millions of dollars, he gave it to someone in need. This man worked for W.L. for less than ten cents on the dollar. If anyone asked him why he gave away such a valuable piece of property by which the sale of said property could sustain him for most of his life, he would tell them that God was the supplier of his needs.

Chapter 2

The Upbringing of Paul

PAUL BAINS WAS THE YOUNGEST member of his family. He was a bundle of energy from the moment he was born. There was a large age gap between him and his oldest sibling. As a result, some of his siblings helped raise him, as they were practically old enough to be his parent. As a child, Paul was like the Energizer Bunny. During his older sister's wedding, he ran around the reception at break-neck speed. He ran into a glass window, fell down, got back up, and continued running. His family has retold this story several times, as it was one of the highlights of his childhood mischievousness. Interestingly, this part of him has not changed. Although you will not find him running around inside of buildings, he is constantly on the run going from one meeting to the next. He does not like being stagnant. He keeps himself busy and is very connected to community leaders, church leaders, and a host of politicians and thought leaders.

Paul was an optimistic, happy go lucky child. His parents endured the unimaginable pain of losing two adolescent children. Prior to Paul's birth, his brother Samuel was hit and killed by a train in a mysterious accident. Saint Samuel Church of God in Christ was named after the precious young son and brother who died such a tragic death. As Paul grew up, he was often told by his siblings, friends, and teachers that he bore some resemblance to his late brother. Samuel was kind, outgoing, helpful, and well- liked by many. Paul has these identical qualities. He goes above and beyond to help people in need. It's as if he feels a personal burden for the struggling and suffering, especially friends and adopted family members. His generosity far exceeds the norm. It is the essence of his character an inseparable core component of his being.

When Paul was four years old his 14-year old sister died of complications caused by sickle cell anemia. Paul remembers attending the funeral and looking up at the casket. He was confused at what was going on around him. He remembers the sad looks on everyone's face, the heartbreak in his mother's eyes and the endless tears. His parents had an inconceivable strength and navigated through these painful experiences. It was their faith in God and the assurance that they would see them again one day that helped them to make it through. Additionally, they did not want their suffering to overshadow their joy, so they persevered.

Despite the sad times, the Bains children have many fond memories of their upbringing. They had family dinners several nights a week where they would gather around the table, talk, laugh, and enjoy the delicious meal prepared by their mother and sisters. Sunday dinners were extra special. W. L. would begin each dinner by reciting the Lord's Prayer. They loved and appreciated one another and were grateful for so many family moments.

W.L. liked to make his wife and children laugh. He loved drinking Slurpee's from 7 Eleven. He would drink them too fast and get 'brain freeze.' Then he would smack the table and say, 'oh my head.' The children thought that was hilarious and still laugh about it when they reflect on the 'good old days.'

Although W.L. had a humorous side, he ran a tight ship. If he told his children to do something, he wasn't going to repeat it. If they did not listen, they were going to be in big trouble. He had a way of looking at the children when they misbehaved that let them know that they needed to straighten up. He held high morals and values and expected his children to abide by these values. For example, he didn't believe in using profanity or anything related to profanity. He was opposed to smoking, drinking, or listening to 'worldly music.' He only allowed for Christian music to be played in the house. He was a strict disciplinarian who believed in corporal punishment. Paul only remembers getting three spankings from his dad. The first one was when he was four years old. He went to the store with his father to purchase something and Paul picked up a package of beef jerky and walked out of the store with it. That is when he learned about stealing and the consequences of taking something in which he did not pay.

Although Paul only received a few spankings from his dad, he received several from his mom. His sisters received several spankings from both of their parents, but Paul managed to learn from their mistakes. W. L. wanted to make sure that his children were prepared for the 'real world,' so he made sure that the children did chores. On Saturdays they had to clean the house from top to bottom. Paul was not a fan of cleaning on Saturday because of course church was on Sunday and they were expected to be at every service. The children were very committed to their church.

The most treasured time of year for the Bains family was Thanksgiving and Christmas. Paul loved the holidays. He lived for them. The Bains family would watch old 8mm movies. The entire family would be over and of course various friends and extended family members. Paul's older brother Richard moved out of the house when he was 18 years old. However, Christmas brought the entire family together. They loved going shopping and especially enjoyed going to the Kress store and shop in San Francisco. They would get in the church van (a van his parents bought but used for the church). W. L. would drive around San Francisco. He was familiar with the different areas of this great city because he worked there.

There was one occasion when Paul was eight or nine years old and the family was doing holiday shopping. While they were in Macy's, Paul was punching on a punching bag, having a wonderful time pretending to be Mohammed Ali. W.L. observed him from afar. He approached Paul and told him to go and check on his mother. This was a diversion tactic because W.L. knew that the punching bag would be the perfect gift for Paul. As Paul reached his mother, he turned around and saw that his dad had the box with the punching bag in his hand. Paul was extremely excited because he knew that he was getting it for Christmas.

Paul loved picking out the tree. At an early age, he considered himself to be a tree decorator extraordinaire. One year his mother picked out the tree and it was a 'Charlie Brown Christmas tree.' It was small and frail and the branches were spread out quite far apart. With childlike optimism, Paul meticulously decorated the tree so even that tree was beautiful. His parents were pleasantly surprised. The things that Paul loved most about Christmas were the beautiful gifts under the freshly decorated tree and the endless food. Also, he loved to buy gifts for family and friends often surprising them with his special presents. He remembers buying his mother two small mirrors with angels on them. He spent all the money he had on this gift and was excited to give it to her. She loved it and hung it in the living room. Each year he bought his father ties and socks. Buying gifts was so foundational for Paul that people made sure he was able to purchase them. This included members of his family and people in the store who were moved that this young man wanted to buy such nice gifts for his parents. Whenever he didn't have enough money, strangers in the store were willing to pitch in to help him purchase the perfect Christmas gift.

His family always had such a wonderful time. They went to church as a family and the children gave Christmas speeches. They sang Christmas music and brought gifts for their extended church family. After church, Paul enjoyed playing with his friends and seeing what gifts his friends got for Christmas. If one of his friends didn't get anything, he liked to share his toys because he always got more than one gift. One thing that he did not enjoy about Christmas, was when he received clothes. He preferred that clothes be given at a less festive occasion.

As his siblings got older, his brother would come and give his father money in a card. This became a family tradition. W.L. would shake the card to see what dropped out. This practice evolved into a game. His older sister would come up with creative ways to give money and make it into a gift. One year she made a tree with dollar bills. Another time she taped the money inside the card so that it would not fall out when he would shake it. It was all done in fun. This tradition added to the joy of the holiday season.

Interestingly, this spirit of giving has continued through Pastor Bains and his family. Christmas at the Bains house is an all-day event with seemingly endless gifts. He spends months purchasing gifts so that his tree is filled with beautiful presents. This writer calls their celebration 'Christmas on Steroids' because it is so extravagant. He is highly generous and sacrifices to make sure that everyone in his family gets something really nice, and hopefully what they want. His wife Cheryl supports this and together they have abundantly provided for not only their family, but many others in the community. They host an annual toy give-away at St. Samuel and give toys and clothing to hundreds of community members in partnership with the police department.

Not only did W. L. teach his children the spirit of giving, but he provided an entrepreneurial platform for his children. This is truly unique, as most children grow up with the mindset of getting a job, not owning their own business. This influence greatly impacted the Bains children to the extent that at some point in each of his children's lives each child owned his or her own business. W.L. came from Texas with two quarters in his pocket. He knew how to earn money and how to survive when things were scarce. He was a strong believer that entrepreneurship was the most effective way for African Americans to level the playing field. He managed to eventually purchase a house in Palo Alto, not far from the esteemed Stanford University.

Paul's oldest brother desired to open a business. His mother helped him purchase his first truck so that he could open a furniture business. Soon thereafter, he realized that he was moving more furniture than he was selling, so he purchased a second truck and started a moving business. Additionally, he helped a close friend start a business. He quickly realized that he had a knack for business and he started investing in real estate. He started small. He bought a house, moved in, built onto the house to add value, and then sold the house. He would reinvest his money into a larger house and follow the same process. He continued doing this with houses and other pieces of real estate. He currently owns a 36-acre ranch and several properties.

Paul became an entrepreneur at an early age. As a child, his father made him earn his own money. In elementary and junior high school, he would buy candy in East Palo Alto and sell it in Palo Alto because Now or Laters candy and certain types of Bazooka gum were not available. In high school, he would sell fireworks purchased from China Town. The Bains family eventually opened two family businesses, *Bains Furniture*, which eventually became *Bains Moving and Storage*, which Paul's older brother opened with his wife. Paul worked in this business for several years. He eventually owned 10% of this business. This became the largest African American moving company in Northern California, with revenues reaching $4,000,000. Paul and Cheryl later opened *Bains Facilities Management* (BFM), which he grew to a $5,000,000 business.

The examples that were modeled for Paul by his oldest brother, as well as the example of W.L. have deeply impacted the belief system of Pastor Bains. He has an optimism that can be somewhat surprising for anyone unfamiliar with his history. For him, obstacles are simply part of the journey that one encounters on their way to success. It is this positive attitude that has launched him forward to multiple successes. He believes that every set-back is a set up for a come-back!

Chapter 3

The Good Thing

'He who finds a wife finds a good thing and obtains favor from the Lord.' Proverbs 18:22 (NIV)

Pastor and Cheryl's wedding

On a cool day in November of 1990, Paul walked into the Church of God in Christ Convocation in Memphis, Tennessee. He had traveled for several hours to attend this convention. This was a large convention for church members from all over the world. Many of the best preachers in the Church of God in Christ would be in attendance. There would be great teaching, powerful music, and the opportunity to catch up with people he had not seen in a while. Paul was no stranger to this setting; it was an annual conference that he thoroughly enjoyed. This particular Convocation would prove to be different than any convention that he had ever attended. As he walked through the vestibule, he took a mental inventory of the various booths. It seemed like every type of Christian product was available for purchase. Paul had saved up money for this occasion. He had no intention of leaving empty handed. As he gazed through the different items available, he noticed one booth where they were selling Christian t-shirts, golf shirts, and other custom made unique items.

He made his way to the booth making sure to walk with the cool swagger that he had rehearsed for several years. He approached the booth, stopped, put his hand in his pocket, smiled at the lovely lady working the booth and said, 'hello.'

'Hi', said the woman with the warm smile and kind eyes as she returned his smile. During this somewhat awkward exchange, the owner of the business, Cheryl, was kneeling underneath the table in which he was standing pulling extra inventory out of the strategically placed boxes, carefully hidden underneath the table cloth. She heard Paul's greeting, looked up at Paul, said, 'hi,' and placed her head back under the table to continue with her task. Paul took offense to her aloofness. He could not understand why she was seemingly too busy to give him the attention to which he was accustomed. He stood in silence for a moment until the other worker, Debby, sensed his agitation and began to engage him in conversation. This turned out to be a wise decision because he purchased a custom shirt designed by Cheryl, but not before making plans to meet the two ladies for dinner.

By the time the Convocation dismissed for the evening, it was after 10 o'clock. The Convocation had been going on all day. Cheryl was exhausted. She was not particularly interested in having dinner with this stranger. She was more interested in putting on her pajamas and watching a little television before drifting off to sleep. Nevertheless, Debby was her sister. She couldn't allow her sister to go out alone with this stranger. She went along, but with inward objections. Cheryl was very quiet at the restaurant while Paul and Debby engaged in a great deal of conversation. Finally Cheryl took it upon herself to take a nap at the table. Curiously, she did not attempt to hide her exhaustion. She actually laid her head on her arm on the table and rested while Debby and Paul conversed. This peaked Paul's interest. After all, he was used to women swooning all over him. Not Cheryl! She didn't seem to take much notice of him at all. With a combination of curiosity and ego, Paul was determined to get Cheryl to notice him.

The next day, he made a special trip to the now familiar booth to say hello. He realized that that effort alone would not be sufficient, so he offered to go and buy them lunch. Surely, being the gentleman that he was, he could not let these two beautiful ladies starve.

'What' would you like to eat? I will bring you anything you want,' he asked Debby while doing his best to avoid eye contact with Cheryl. 'Shrimp,' she replied, 'Then shrimp it is,' he said. Cheryl shook her head in disbelief. She didn't believe for a moment that Paul was going to buy them shrimp. She made a groaning sound which Paul took as a personal challenge.

As he walked away, he began to have a dialogue in his head. He could not believe the nerve of Cheryl to doubt him. "Who did she think she was?" "Why was she so mean?" He wondered if she thought that he couldn't afford shrimp?

Little did he know that shrimp would be nearly impossible to procure in that area of Memphis. He was not one to fold under a challenge. He spent over an hour driving around on the hunt for shrimp. Finally, he found a bar that sold shrimp. By the time he returned to the Convocation, he was late for his session and aggravated. He sat the shrimp down in front of the ladies and walked away, glaring the entire time. He made a point to make eye contact with Cheryl to make sure that she understood that he proved her wrong. He felt personal satisfaction knowing that he had shown her. His determination would have caused him to go to the grocery store, rent a kitchen and make the shrimp, had he been unsuccessful in finding it. How dare she challenge him!

After this incident, Debby and Paul became good friends. He still had not successfully peaked Cheryl's interest. This now became a challenge, an obstacle if you will. He realized that he was spending more time than usual thinking about her and he didn't even have her phone number. He had to come up with a plan to get in touch with her. During his next conversation with Debby, he explained to Debby that he was interested in purchasing more shirts from Cheryl. He sheepishly asked if he could get her business number. Debby was oblivious to his true motive and gave Paul the number. This was in February. He called Cheryl and placed an order. This was a small price to pay to get her phone number. He began to call Cheryl regularly with no intention of purchasing additional merchandise.

When Cheryl met Paul, she had recently experienced her own heart break. She was not interested in dating anyone. Paul continued to call. He would frequently call during her favorite television shows, so she would half talk to him while watching her shows. She informed him that this was not the best time to call. He continued to call during that time, as it was convenient for him. This went on for four months. Finally, Paul got tired of the 'cold shoulder.' He decided that he had invested enough of his time in this woman who was seemingly impossible to get. He decided to never call her again. After about a week of no phone calls, Cheryl realized that Paul was not calling her at all. She didn't like the thought that she might not hear from him again. After all, she was fond of that cute little dimple on his right cheek. She decided to make a bold move and conjure up all the nerve that she could and gave him a call. He was both shocked and excited to hear from her.

After that treasured phone call, Cheryl paid a lot less attention to television and a lot more attention to Paul's conversation. Paul's excitement and interest continued to grow as the conversations became more frequent. His nephew was taking a trip to Atlanta, so he arranged a meeting between his nephew and Cheryl. They met and had polite conversation. His nephew liked Cheryl and felt that she was very nice and beautiful so he gave Paul the 'thumbs up.'

Cheryl was in an intensive Bible program with her church. She was studying leadership. She shared with Paul the wonderful things that she was learning and the innovative ministries of her church. Paul used this opportunity to invite her to come to California as a guest speaker at his family church. During the summer, she came and spoke at the church. Paul had forgot just how beautiful she was in person. He could barely take his eyes off her. As she spoke, he was impressed with her knowledge and abilities. She did an excellent job communicating her message, which impressed him even more. He was not going to risk losing her. She was indeed a keeper. He made sure that on this trip that they made their relationship official. He could now let everyone know that she was his girlfriend.

The relationship continued to be long distance. They talked on the phone several times a week. They prayed for and with each other and encouraged one another. The bond continued to get closer and 'lo and behold' Paul and Cheryl fell in love. Several months after their reunion, Paul realized that he couldn't live without Cheryl, so he contacted her parents to get permission to propose. When he asked for her hand she gave an emphatic yes and began to plan her wedding. They made the decision together that she would move to California. She packed up her belongings in November and relocated to California. Paul and Cheryl were married in April of 1992.

Paul is not one for small gestures, so he planned a dream honeymoon. This dream trip consisted of Niagara Falls, a visit to her family home in Ohio for a wedding reception given by Cheryl's parents, and then a surprise vacation to Hawaii. Planning special trips for one another became an integral part of their love story. Each year Cheryl plans an exciting get away for Paul's birthday. He never knows where they are going or what surprises await him.

This year they celebrated their 25th anniversary. Paul spent almost a year planning the perfect 2nd honeymoon. He took her on a three-week surprise vacation which started off with a 12 day five island Hawaiian cruise! After the cruise, he took her to Vancouver, British Columbia for two days, Niagara Falls for three days, and then they went to visit her mother and sister in Ohio. It was a reverse trip from their original honeymoon.

Paul and Cheryl have three beautiful daughters. The oldest two were diagnosed with Sickle Cell Anemia, a debilitating disease which resulted in many hospital visits, monthly blood transfusions, and unimaginable pain. Cheryl and Paul provide enormous support to their children. The obstacle of illness is ongoing, but they are grateful. This experience has given them strength and resiliency which has brought them closer than they ever dreamt possible.

Pastor and Cheryl Bains

Chapter 4

All Can Win

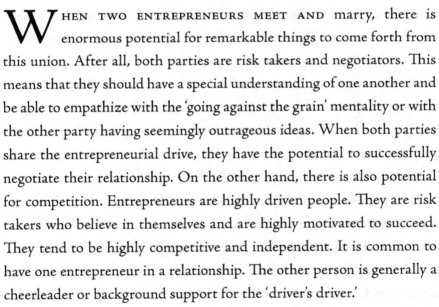

W HEN TWO ENTREPRENEURS MEET AND marry, there is enormous potential for remarkable things to come forth from this union. After all, both parties are risk takers and negotiators. This means that they should have a special understanding of one another and be able to empathize with the 'going against the grain' mentality or with the other party having seemingly outrageous ideas. When both parties share the entrepreneurial drive, they have the potential to successfully negotiate their relationship. On the other hand, there is also potential for competition. Entrepreneurs are highly driven people. They are risk takers who believe in themselves and are highly motivated to succeed. They tend to be highly competitive and independent. It is common to have one entrepreneur in a relationship. The other person is generally a cheerleader or background support for the 'driver's driver.'

When both parties are entrepreneurs, competition can easily invade a relationship because both people have the mind of a mogul. One reason why things can get competitive is because entrepreneurs play to win. On one hand, this is a great characteristic. Winning is a good thing. The problem that can arise when both people are supposed to be on the same team is that when partners play to win, one person loses. How can one team be winning and losing at the same time? It goes directly against the definition and concept of team work.

In a marriage, unity is the goal. Competitive people don't generally set out to be divisive. They get caught up in the excitement of winning. Competition, even friendly competition excites them. They are naturally competitive and independent. Keep in mind, Cheryl Bains successfully started and operated her own Christian t-shirt company. She created and designed her shirts, ordered embroidered items, arranged opportunities to market and sell her items, and handled the banking and accounting. She was well educated, having graduated from Clark University, a well-esteemed historically black university. Additionally, she had extensive training on leadership through intensive programs at her highly established church. She entered this union with a wealth of knowledge, determination, and eagerness to make an impact on a community in need. She was driven, accomplished, and competitive. She was not a background person. She was a natural born leader. She entered into this partnership feeling as if her education, upbringing and experience prepared for her such a time as this. She was ready to make her mark in the world.

Her mother is a godly woman who raised her in the church. She is a well-respected church mother and national evangelist who preaches, teaches, and prays. She is considered a 'prayer warrior' in her church circle. She is very powerful and dynamic, yet meek and humble at the same time. Cheryl grew up with this excellent role model. Further she was highly involved in her church in Atlanta, Georgia. She worked alongside several well-known pastors and teachers. She is the youngest child in her family who possesses confidence and boldness and knows how to assert herself.

However, Paul was the youngest child of eight. His older siblings were exceptionally outgoing. One of his sisters was remarkably bold and taught him how to be comfortable approaching and befriending people in a way in which most people are unfamiliar. He is extremely assertive, passionate and tenacious. He mastered the art of persuasiveness at an early age. He is an independent, confident non-conformist.

Both Paul and Cheryl are goal oriented and each had a fighter's instinct. Just imagine these two strong personalities coming together. It could have played out in multiple different scenarios. Additionally, both came from families with strong personalities and intense leadership characteristics. If they did not learn how to work together, this could have been a battle ground, each person striving to outdo the other. They both have multiple skill sets that were generally in the forefront.

Some people find themselves in a relationship like this and they feel insecure and think they must prove their worth to the other person. This can be in a business relationship, friendship, or romantic involvement. When this happens, things can quickly deteriorate. After all, a two-headed leader is a monster. In this union, Cheryl assumed more of a background role, so there was support instead of competitiveness. She could have taken a different type of role and made sure that she received the proper accolades for her contributions, however, she could see the bigger picture. She understood the importance of unity and harmony and recognized her value. This enabled her to provide the proper support to her husband and insure that business was headed in the right direction. Their marriage was healthy and everyone was content. Bains Facilities Management was profitable. In 1998, they purchased the Bains family home in Palo Alto and were doing a massive remodel. Their daughter's health was stable and the church was continuing to grow. W.L. had passed away a few years prior, so they were mourning their loss and picking up the pieces. Additionally, Paul's mother's health was declining. Despite any areas of struggle, they were a solid unit.

Having two entrepreneurial spirits occupy the same space does not have to become an obstacle. It can become a strength providing that the two parties communicate with each other effectively and each person discovers their role. When this happens, a dynamic duo is birthed, as was the case with Paul and Cheryl.

Prior to getting married, Paul and Cheryl attended pre-marital counseling. They discovered that they both had a desire to help people. Cheryl was interested in opening a community center to address the needs of the most vulnerable members of the community. Paul wanted to help homeless and youth. Paul had this desire because his parents always helped people. That was something that Paul deeply admired about his father. Further, his mother would cook meals and deliver them to the elderly.

Pastor Bains was an avid viewer of Tele-evangelist Carlton Pearson. He appreciated the things that Carlton did in the community and desired to give back in a comparable way. On one occasion while he was watching Carlton Pearson on television it was announced he was hosting a conference in Oklahoma. Paul discussed the upcoming conference with Cheryl and they made the decision to attend. They flew to Oklahoma and were inspired by all the churches and ministries that were present. This conference included many people making a difference in varying communities all throughout the country. This conference, *Church Agency Development,* changed the direction of their ministry. It caused them to think about outreach in a broader way. They made the decision to travel to different states and observe the work of some of the other people who also attended the conference. They were determined to witness their impacts first hand. Upon returning from this trip, they decided to cast a new vision for Saint Samuel Church.

There were no losers. The couple learned that when they worked together not only would they win, but their community could win. When people come together, it is amazing how many remarkable things can happen. Unfortunately, they found that some people do not always operate within the bounds of unity. When this happens, division or competition can become an obstacle. It causes people to compete with one another instead of working together. This is a waste of time and resources. Communities have non-profit organizations who are doing the same thing rather than complimenting each other. Instead of working together they attempt to undermine and sabotage each other. In fact, this is counterproductive when trying to help a community. It can take the focus away from the issue and place it on the division. Whereas collaboration helps churches, nonprofits, etc. better utilize their resources. It heightens their credibility and it can be leveraged in multiple ways.

Chapter 5

The Birth of Project WeHOPE

AFTER RETURNING FROM A HIGHLY productive trip where they witnessed firsthand the benefit of collaboration, Pastor Bains and Cheryl decided to open a non-profit with a separate tax id number from Saint Samuel Church. They decided that they wanted to do something that was a community benefit and a direct social service which would impact the lives of people even if they were not people of faith. They felt that this would be the most practical approach because of 'separation of church and state.' He knew that he wanted to use the word 'hope' as part of the name because they both desired to bring hope to the world. Additionally, he likes acronyms so he had a desire to incorporate an acronym into the name. They sat down individually and wrote down different possible names. They came together and presented the names to one another. The name 'WeHOPE' stuck out for both of them.

Cheryl immediately began researching the process. She then completed the necessary paperwork. She drew up the bylaws and worked with their existing business attorney to fully develop their non-profit. Cheryl is meticulous and made sure that everything was established correctly. Interestingly, the organization was established to be a combination of each of the original visions that they discussed during pre-marital counseling. It was also determined that Project WeHOPE would be located in East Palo Alto.

East Palo Alto has a unique history. It was originally a part of unincorporated San Mateo County, founded in 1849. It is a small community, approximately 2.4 square miles, with a lot of character. This charming city did not have official boundaries until 1983 when it was officially incorporated. The original inhabitants of this petite city were Ohlone/Costanoan Native Americans. As time progressed, Spanish ranchers made their way to this quaint town. Then Caucasians began to settle here, followed by Asians and Pacific Islanders. It eventually became the largest African American community on the Peninsula. It is a racially diverse community with a population of approximately 29,000 (www.ci.east-palo-alto.ca).

In 1992, East Palo Alto was once known as the 'murder capital' per capita. Times have changed and so has the reputation of this multi-ethnic city located in the booming Silicon Valley. On one side of East Palo Alto sits that very wealthy city of Palo Alto, while on the other side lies Menlo Park, the new home of Facebook. East Palo Alto has worked to change its reputation, and in many respects, has successfully done so. However, due to the poverty rate, crime rate, disproportionate homeless population, and lack of affordable housing, many people in the Bay Area are afraid to visit this city.

Interestingly, many Californians are attracted to East Palo Alto because of the beautiful San Francisco Bay Area weather, the affordable land, as compared to other cities on the Peninsula, the stunning view, centralized location and accessibility to public transportation. Pastor Bains lived in this city for many years and it grew on him. He purchased two homes in the city limits and enjoyed getting to know the community. He developed a deep affection for the people and the culture it provided. He recognized some of the injustices that were taking place and desired to be part of the solution. The Bains family developed a good reputation in East Palo Alto because they were the largest private employer of all African Americans and Latinos in the city.

In the early 70's, East Palo Alto became a thriving city of strong Black families. Then crack took over and Black males quickly succumbed to this hideous addiction. Families were being destroyed left and right. At the same time, there were issues with some of the local police officers. There was a police group called the "wolfpack," who was using excessive force and violating the trust that they are supposed to uphold. During this time, there were three main territories: The Village, The Gardens, and Midtown. There was a feeling of hopelessness that was sweeping throughout the community. Surprisingly, there were just eight families causing most of the violence in the three territories through drug trafficking and drug related violent crime. Being that East Palo Alto was a very poor city, the City was issued a lot of grant funding. Unfortunately, the grants that were acquired were not trickling down into the community to initiate the needed changes to transform the community.

To provide hope and improve the reputation of their city, Pastor Paul and Cheryl intervened. Through their moving and facilities management companies, Paul and Cheryl knew a lot of people. In other words, they had 'street connections' because they hired people with diverse backgrounds to work for their company to provide a 'second chance'. They liked to solve problems no matter how complex and desired to bridge the gap between the 'haves and the have nots.' Pastor Bains grew up in Palo Alto and East Palo Alto so he had the best of both worlds. He knew a variety of people from different ethnicities which helped him communicate and share the vision with many different people by different means.

Project WeHOPE started in 1999 with a couple of primary programs for youth. The first program that was implemented was called *STAND* which stood for Students Taking A New Direction. This program was created to combat truancy in public schools. It was a program that operated during the school day to provide an alternative to home suspension. This comprehensive intervention program was designed by Cheryl. She had a burning desire to help the youth who were kicked out of class. She felt that they needed the opportunity to receive tutoring instead of going home, sitting in the office, or getting involved in truancy. The original intention was for this program to operate in East Palo Alto, but the local school district was not receptive to it. Therefore, the initial program operated in Santa Clara County on one campus; however, it supported three high schools and three middle schools. It is important to note that this happened during a time when there were not a lot of after-school programs operating in California, so Project WeHOPE was one of the first. This program successfully ran for five years. During this time, over 10,000 children were serviced. Further, to coincide with this successful program, they developed the SUCCEED Debutante Program which ran for two-years. It provided college scholarships to graduating at-risk high school girls.

Another program that was developed during the embryo stages of Project WeHOPE was the House of Hope. This was a transitional house established to reduce recidivism and assist homeless men. It also focused on prison re-entry. House of Hope was launched because Pastor Bains owned a house in East Palo Alto and wanted to use it to assist homeless adult males. He noticed a gap in services for this population and wanted to do his part to help. This program provided a safe place, reduced recidivism, taught responsibility and helped men learn to own their own destiny. The overarching goal was to encourage the residents to attend junior college or attend a trade school to help them become gainfully employed. This program was self-funded by Pastor and Cheryl Bains without the benefit of grants or other outside funding.

House of Hope had the capacity for 10 males and it was filled. Paul and Cheryl spent thousands of dollars of their own money to remodel the house. Additionally, a couple of local nonprofit organizations assisted with some of the needed remodeling. Unfortunately, due to an economic crisis and predatory lending practices, Pastor and Cheryl Bains lost the house to foreclosure. It was a very painful experience. Despite this difficult setback, they kept pressing forward. Their desire to make a difference did not diminish. They decided to re-group and continue to help the less fortunate. Instead of focusing on themselves they recognized that even though they had this setback, they were still blessed and continued to fulfill their vision.

In 2004, Project WeHOPE partnered with the East Palo Alto Police Department to start the Chaplaincy Program. Paul recognized that law enforcement and the community were not seeing 'eye to eye.' More specifically most people of color did not trust the police and feared them due to the residual damage from the 'wolfpack.' Pastor Bains felt it was his responsibility to bridge the gap between the police and the community. He believed that being a pastor placed him in a unique position to help institute change and to be an agent of peace. He helped the police to better understand and work with the community by providing opportunities for open dialogue between the police and the community.

The program started off with seven chaplains in East Palo Alto. It extended to Palo Alto, Mountainview, and Menlo Park and is still highly active. Currently there is a much higher level of trust between the police and the community. Police officers volunteer at Project WeHOPE's annual Thanksgiving and Christmas banquets. The police serve dinner to the residents and enjoy pleasant conversation. As of August of 2017, the 'murder capital' has had no murders this year. This drastic change is a partial result of new strategies that police have implemented as well as partnerships with community and faith based organizations.

In 2008, Project WeHOPE launched a midnight soccer and midnight basketball program to help eradicate gang violence in the community. This program successfully helped the local warring factions solve their issues on the basketball courts instead of with bullets. Pastor Bains and Cheryl enjoyed seeing these opposing groups come together and get to know one another. Relations began to improve because they mixed up the teams. In other words, opposing gang members played on the same team instead of against each other. Pastor Bains developed this concept and this practice created team spirit by intertwining the teams. Project WeHOPE was also able to reduce the guns on the streets. As a result of these efforts, some people who needed to leave the community left, which was of great benefit to the community. This has had a significant impact in the reduction of gang violence in the community.

Further, East Palo Alto did not have a local community center, so Project WeHOPE opened their gym to host community events including meetings, dance offs, and spoken-word forums. Word continued to spread about this space which is known as The Lord's Gym. Donations of exercise equipment, a basketball floor, basketball hoops, etc. have been made available to the community. Another local non-profit has begun using the gym to hold basketball practices for youth. Project WeHOPE clearly met a crucial need in the community.

Chapter 6

A Renewed Vision

I N 2009 PASTOR BAINS WAS walking to his office when something caught his eye. His office was located in a warehouse building that housed multiple non-profit organizations. As he approached the door he took notice of a bicycle locker right next to the door. There was a pillow and blanket neatly tucked inside the locker. Pastor Bains stared in disbelief. He realized that someone was sleeping in front of his office. His heart was touched with compassion. He began to reflect on the reality that there were numerous people in the community who needed help in several ways. The blanket and pillow became a visual expression of homelessness that shook him to his core. As the day went on, he kept visualizing that pillow. He felt compelled to do something about it. He spoke to his wife and the Project WeHOPE board members. Together they decided that the homelessness part of the mission needed to come to the forefront. They began to research and discovered that East Palo Alto had the highest rate of homelessness in the County of San Mateo, per capita. The realization provided the motivation to be pioneers addressing this pertinent issue in their community.

For at least five years, East Palo Alto had a community of homeless people who built makeshift huts in marsh land fields which became known as *The Field of Dreams*. There were homeless adults residing there for years, some as many as 12- years. The latest Homeless Census (2015) showed that East Palo Alto had 222 literally homeless individuals. This was an extremely high number considering the size of the city. Another local pastor from East Palo Alto had a strong burden for the homeless in her community. She was instrumental in being a champion for the cause of the homeless assisting in organizing some of the meetings and assuring that the homeless had a voice in the community. She then started working alongside Pastor and Cheryl Bains to help get the attention of those positioned to help.

There are distinct types of people in the world – pioneers and settlers. Pioneers tend to be very optimistic because they can see a problem and muster up a determination to do something about it. A pioneer is a person who is willing to explore and investigate a situation for a purpose. Sometimes the motive of the pioneer can be highly selfish. Other times it can be to add benefit. Pastor and Cheryl Bains were and continue to be pioneers for the disenfranchised members of East Palo Alto. They have a unique compassion to reach the least and the lost and to help restore them. This is one of the many reasons why they became ministers of Saint Samuel Church. They love people and believe there is hope regardless of the situation in which one finds him or herself. I looked in the Thesaurus to find some alternate words for pioneer and the ones that stuck out for me were innovator, creator, discoverer, and go out in front. Project WeHOPE seeks to be a pioneer in developing a model homeless shelter. The staff literally goes out in front creating programs and processes that increase the quality of life for the hungry and homeless.

With prayer, drive, ambition, and determination, Pastor and Cheryl Bains forged ahead with the approval of their board of directors, church, and close friends. This was a renewed direction for their organization, but they felt led to take on this arduous task. The homeless had quickly resurfaced as part of their personal burden and the only way to lift the burden was to once again do something to help. Sitting around discussing the situation, having political forums, writing blogs, and anything short of being a tangible solution was not sufficient to release the burden that they now carried. Instead they gathered a task force of several local non-profits, shelters, and churches. They collectively formulated a plan, purchased the necessary equipment, and started discussing guidelines. These meetings began in late February and they desired to open the doors in November of 2009 to the first and only emergency warming shelter in East Palo Alto and one of only three emergency shelters in the entire County of San Mateo.

Chapter 7

Bumps and Bruises

T HE MONEY WAS NOT THERE, but the determination and drive were ever- present. Even when you want to do something good for the community, there will still be obstacles that will seem to come out of nowhere. Many people fold under these obstacles. They look at resistance as a "no" from God or the universe. Pastor Bains was not going to give up just because circumstances became difficult. He once told me, 'If I went by no's, BFM never would've started; Project WeHOPE would not be in existence today. We wouldn't have a shelter. I believe in 'no' when God says 'no', not when man says no.' This is the level of strength that it takes to keep pushing. Many people are not visionaries. They believe that everyone should live in the same type of invisible box that they live in. Ironically, sometimes these same people find themselves in positions of power and stifle the growth of others. I don't believe this is always intentional, though sometimes it is.

For Project WeHOPE, the first obstacle of opening a shelter came with finding the right people to engage in the planning process. Pastor Bains is unique. He understood that he didn't have to have the entire pie; he was more than welcome to share. With that in mind, he gathered a few church leaders, community leaders, political figures, and business professionals. He presented the vision and collaborated with the group to help it come into fruition. Some were excited to help with this project. They were willing to give their meaningful advice and influence on this new project to help it get the best possible start. Others scoffed at the idea and felt that it was impossible. Then there were those that tried to sabotage the project all together. Regardless of the opposition, Pastor Bains and his supporters continued to forge ahead.

As the group assembled, the initial obstacle that blocked progression was the location of the building they were currently using. It was not zoned to be a shelter. This posed a severe problem because they did not have the time nor the resources to find another building or pay rent on two buildings. It seemed they had hit a dead end.

Many would have given up right there because dealing with cities and zoning can be quite complicated. Some of the team members were encouraging him to throw in the towel, while others were loyal to their city and the community members who were suffering. They were willing to do whatever was necessary to open the shelter. Through brainstorming and seeking counsel, they found a loophole. This loophole enabled them to get a conditional use permit. They spoke with the City Planning Commission and were able to streamline the process. Now, they had the building and things seemed to automatically move in a positive direction. Of course, just like in life, when things seem to be going well, another test is right around the corner.

The next obstacle was financial. Opening a shelter was not something Project WeHOPE saved and planned for over a long period of time. There was not a capital campaign or time for a major fundraiser. *Go Fund Me* was not around and so their options seemed limited. Pastor Bains went to San Mateo County and petitioned the County to help the homeless in East Palo Alto. He presented a compelling case. At that time, East Palo Alto had the highest rate of unhoused individuals per capita in San Mateo County. The Director of the Homeless Services Agency heard what Project WeHOPE was doing, saw the need and was determined to help. They had already missed the standard grant cycle, but she could and did commit $30,000 from unused San Mateo County shelter designated funding to assist in this pilot program. Once the County was committed, Pastor Bains approached the East Palo Alto City Council and they committed $30,000 to provide shelter for disenfranchised members of the community. That was all the money they had to buy cots, supplies, hire staff, pay rent, provide food, and fully operate for four months. They were scheduled to open in just a few short months. The newly established board breathed a sigh of relief. They realized that this dream was quickly becoming a reality.

As the team began to evaluate their progress and the things that still needed to be prepared, they realized that there were no policies in place. Not only that, but a training program had not been established. How on earth were they going to pull this off with such a short timeline? They worked tirelessly gathering information from other shelters in San Mateo and Santa Clara Counties. Pastor Bains found a good friend in one of the top administrators in a shelter that served both San Mateo and Santa Clara Counties. Dr. Greenberg was willing to assist the administration and train the staff. Further, several other people in San Mateo County with a wealth of experience were willing to partner with Project WeHOPE and provide a hand up. The excitement in Pastor Bains and the board was contagious. They continued to work with optimism with a surety that the shelter would open on time. One of the local pastors and board members brought a community member who was willing to manage the shelter. This community member loved East Palo Alto and had the passion to help. A wage was negotiated and they began both the tactical and strategic processes. Community members seemingly came out of the woodwork and were willing to volunteer to oversee the shelter clients. Others volunteered to cook and provide meals.

Community members went to the local encampments and informed the many homeless residents that a new shelter was opening in their city. Some of the individuals dwelling in the encampments seemed receptive. They were willing to check it out. Others were not interested from the beginning. Shelters are often viewed as something negative by the homeless. They feel like other people are attempting to infringe their rules on them. Many homeless adults enjoy the opportunity to be independent and make their own decisions independently of the philosophy of the government or a well-meaning agency. Further, some people find peace and serenity in nature. They feel a special connection and enjoy being in the openness of God's creation. This became an additional obstacle.

In February of 2009, Pastor and Cheryl Bains were in the middle of a financial crisis. The change in trends related to facilities management caused them to shut down their business which was their primary source of income. The bills were piling up and the church offerings were declining. Pastor Bains was working with his mortgage company to try and save his family home. In the meantime, he was doing odd jobs to secure the money he needed to save his home. During this stressful time, he kept telling his family that God would make a way. A way was made! Pastor and Cheryl Bains, with the help of the faith-based community, secured the money to stop the foreclosure.

Finally, it was time to open the shelter. Someone painted a tent sign with the words, "Warming Shelter." The sign was placed by the sidewalk to notify the community that the shelter was now open. With anticipation and fear, the shelter opened its doors. The first night seven people showed up. There was space for 40 and only seven showed. The volunteers did their first seven intakes waiting and hoping that more people in need would come and take advantage of this new resource. It didn't happen. They served the nice meal with all the hospitality they could muster while trying to disguise their disappointment. They encouraged each other with words like, "This is just the first day." "Tomorrow will be better." With both enthusiasm and trepidation, they prepared for day two. They kept looking out the door for the crowd to come and utilize their services. The crowd did not come. They quickly realized that they were not going to get the crowds that they wanted right away so they decided to use the leverage that they had to "sell" others who desperately needed their services.

Within a few weeks, they doubled their count. Word started to get around about the low-barrier shelter and the great meals. More homeless men and women decided to check it out. Before long, Project WeHOPE began partnering with CORE service agencies in San Mateo County. These agencies started sending referrals to the new shelter. During the first season, they peaked at 15 people in a single night. This number does not include the one time or few time users. Excitement grew amongst the team as the numbers increased. They had a group of regular users who started to feel like the shelter was their refuge. At last, they were making progress and feeling like they were making the difference that they intended to make. Then, the inclement weather season was over and the clients were scheduled to return to homelessness. Suddenly, the excitement turned to despair. The group began to wonder if they were accomplishing what they intended. Discussions erupted regarding ways to keep the clients in the shelter. There was no more money and they had to close. The clients did not want to leave and the team did not want them to go. Unfortunately, they did not have a choice, so the shelter closed until the next season.

The 2010/2011 season started with excitement and anticipation. The Project WeHOPE Board remained intact and they continued to strategize and figure out ways that they could increase the shelter usage and open year-round. They celebrated a successful year. They approached the County and the City, but neither had the funding to help them open a year-round shelter. They concluded that they had to remain an inclement weather shelter because at least the homeless would have a place to go during the lowest temperatures and rainy nights. Once again, they enlisted volunteers, churches, community groups, and any good Samaritan who was willing to share their time, talent, and treasure with the most vulnerable members of our community. Things got off to a bit of a slow start, but they picked up much faster this year. After all, they already had a group of people excited to receive shelter. At the end of March, it was time to close the doors again. Unavoidably, the prior cycle repeated itself.

In 2011/2012 things were steadily picking up. Police were dropping off clients, churches started calling to make sure they could send clients over, and other San Mateo County agencies were alerted of the shelter services. That year Project WeHOPE secured a little more funding to provide stipends for the workers. During the first couple of years of the shelter being in operation, Pastor Bains did not receive a salary. He was more concerned with everyone else getting paid. He appreciated their hearts to serve and wanted to reward them in any and every way that he could. Some of the people who had previously volunteered appreciated the blessing.

Unfortunately, during 2011, one of the board members did not agree with some of the organizational and operational decisions that were taking place. They decided to leave the board. Pastor Bains and Cheryl understood their decision. They did not have any hard feelings towards the person who faithfully served and decided to move on. They didn't believe in burning bridges, so they left the door open for that person to return if they so desired. At the same time, a transition was taking place and the shelter manager moved on to another local organization.

While preparing for the 2012/2013 season, Pastor Bains and Cheryl realized they needed to bring an additional administrator to the team to help it grow and align with the vision they had for the shelter. They needed someone with business experience and with organization skills. They approached me and asked me to come as an interim Operations Manager to help get the business better organized and function more efficiently by developing and implementing systems and processes. The plan was for me to come for about a year, two at the most and use my education and skills to help the company grow. I was excited to come on board and utilize my education, knowledge, experience and skills. The idea that it was a short-term project was very attractive to me. I had been working for the same company for 10 years, so this was a welcome change of pace. My goal was to work for them for a year or two and then pursue being an elementary school principal. Prior to starting, I began researching grant opportunities because having worked for other non-profit organizations, I knew that funding was always an obstacle. Cheryl and I completed four grants. We were awarded two of the four. Also, one of the grant makers gave us $5000 more than our request. What an exciting way to begin a new job! I realized that the blessings of God were in this organization and I was eager to play a part.

During that same year, San Mateo County sent a Request for Proposal for a large grant that would help the shelter open year-round. We applied for this grant and were awarded $1.2 million dollars over the next two years. This would be paid out at $700,000 for the first year ($200,000 in start-up costs) and $500,000 for the following year. The level of excitement felt can hardly be articulated in words. We stood in awe over the blessings of God and realized the difference we would be able to make in the lives of our clients and staff. My first real order of business was to hire staff. There were already several people who had previously volunteered or received a small stipend. They were hired with a salary above minimum wage. We brought in a few new people to cover shifts and training began.

During the first four years of Project WeHOPE Shelter, we had two restrooms for client use and no showers or laundry capabilities. The shelter opened at 8:30 PM and closed at 8:30 AM. It operated like a typical emergency shelter where the clients lined up outside the front door waiting for the shelter to open. When we opened the first night of the 2012/2013 season, we had 12 clients. They came in, we gave them a hot meal, and they prepared to go to sleep. They woke up at 6:30 in the morning, had a continental breakfast, and went about their day. It was a pretty good operation. The staff was well trained and carried out their responsibilities professionally.

Our objective was to keep homeless men and women from San Mateo County off the street for safety purposes and human dignity. Many studies have concluded that the life expectancy of a housed individual far exceeds the life expectancy of a homeless individual. Moreover, there are various personal safety concerns. Therefore, providing shelter is both a social justice and moral obligation.

The primary concern when I started was the shelter utilization rate. We had a contract with San Mateo County to shelter 40 people a night. We realized that we would have to increase our outreach efforts to fulfill our contract. Most of the original clients who came to the shelter were from East Palo Alto and East Menlo Park. For four years we served primarily this demographic, with others coming from neighboring cities in San Mateo County as well as a small percentage of people coming from Santa Clara County. Our outreach efforts included going to local encampments, making new referral forms and distributing them to various agencies who engage with the homeless throughout the entire County. Within a few weeks, we were at the maximum nightly capacity.

Word got out to different agencies throughout the County that our low-barrier shelter had beds available. People from various cities throughout the County received referrals and came to stay in the shelter. This upset some of the local clients and community members. They felt that they were being slighted. In other words, they were used to having East Palo Alto and East Menlo Park residents occupy the shelter. These communities are extremely close-knit, so they knew one another and felt comfortable with each other. People they did not know and whom they considered to be 'outsiders' were now occupying the same space. They began to feel as if the shelter was being taken over.

We started having weekly meetings with the clients to give them an opportunity to express themselves in a respectful way. This helped mitigate the situation. Additionally, we explained to the clients and the concerned community members that the majority of our funding was provided by grants from San Mateo County. We were expected to accept clients from the entire County. We reached a certain level of understanding which improved the shelter environment.

Inclement weather persisted several nights during this season and the capacity was increased by adding 20 additional cots. Inclement weather nights were particularly stressful because we had only two client restrooms for up to 60 people. The clients were gracious and worked towards sharing the space equitably.

During the 2012/2013 season, Habitat for Humanity and Rebuilding Together selected Project WeHOPE for a large renovation project because of the large impact the organization was making in the community. This was particularly exciting because this meant that we would be able to add a small kitchen, conference room, an upstairs storage space, two washers, two dryers, two handicap accessible restrooms as well as two handicap accessible showers. Not only did they have professional contractors and community volunteers working on the project, but they also provided the equipment. This was a wonderful season of growth for Project WeHOPE. This enabled us to provide several essential services to our clients. At the same time, preparation for additional expansion in operations were worked on, as the funds were scheduled for the 2013/2014 fiscal year. There was now the option to close on March 30 or take a leap of faith and remain open without having enough funding for operations and staffing. If the latter option was selected, our clients would once again be without shelter until July 1st.

Pastor Bains decided that the shelter would go ahead and remain open. Doing so depleted all our reserve funding. The projected budget showed that if everything went as planned, we would barely be able to make it. At the beginning of July, we waited for the start-up cost funds to hit our account. Our bank accounts were nearly at a zero balance. There were a few hold ups with the funds and we became concerned. Payroll was approaching and we did not have enough money to make payroll. Once again, there was pressure of how dire the situation was. We had 12 employees and 50 clients who were depending on us. We started to pray for guidance and God's provision. It seemed like the more we prayed, the longer the delay was extended for the check.

At this point we needed to access our social capital. Social capital are the people that you know with wealth, influence, and compassion. They can assist when you find yourself in a seemingly impossible situation. Pastor Bains is one of the most well-connected people that I know. He has a lot of friends with money and influence. He realized how dire the situation was so he made a few phone calls for help. One of his long- time friends provided financial assistance through an emergency grant which carried us through a few weeks. August came and our account was once again getting exceptionally low. Not only that, but we found out that the check that we were waiting for was going to be delayed at least another 30 days. Pastor Bains put in a call to another social resource. We received an emergency loan in the amount of $100,000 with zero interest, payable once the grant from the County arrived.

Our contract with San Mateo County required us to open earlier in the evening than we had in previous years. This meant that during this financial hardship we had to hire additional staff and extend our operating hours. In other words, this meant more money had to be paid out. Our new operating hours became 4:30 PM to 8:00 AM. We hired and trained the additional staff members and waited semi-patiently for the funding to arrive. It seemed like the check was never coming. Finally, after an additional 30-day delay, the long-awaited check arrived. Once the check cleared the bank, the first thing we did was pay off the loan. We felt a profound sense of relief because the loan payoff was behind schedule. The lender had been notified in advance and was very understanding. Also, the County was kind enough to write a letter on our behalf to explain the unanticipated delay.

After the loan was paid off, we could procure much needed equipment. Our tables and chairs were falling apart and were becoming ergonomically unsafe. The broken items were recycled and replaced. Broken things around the shelter were fixed, new cots and blankets were purchased and some of our shelving units were replaced.

Around this time our new construction was complete. This happened just in time for our annual Homeless Connect event hosted at the shelter. This is a one-day event where approximately 25 service providers from the area provide on-site services to the homeless, and those at risk of becoming homeless. A hot breakfast, lunch, raffle prizes, showers, backpacks, socks, and various other items are provided to the homeless. In the past, shower units were rented to provide showers for the community. This time we could provide onsite showers and laundry service. The joy of opening our new space was overwhelming. Through extensive outreach efforts, around 150 people attended this event. It was festive and highly motivating. It was exciting to see so many people connected to much needed services.

'This is the greatest day that I have had since being in the shelter,' said a long-time client. People were anxious to use the new showers and washers and dryers. Service providers gave away multiple needed items and provided services directly to the people who needed them. There were not excessive lines which meant It was not necessary to take a number. It was a highly productive day which further introduced our services to our community and met multiple needs of our clients.

Many people do not realize how difficult it is for homeless individuals to access services. This is because many social service agencies are not within close proximity to each other. This causes long bus rides. Simply going to one appointment can take all day. Oftentimes once the person has waited for 2 -3 hours to receive the service, he or she is told that they are missing a document and must come back tomorrow. This causes extreme frustration and humiliation. It can also cause the person to lose motivation to try, especially when the service provider is rude or curt.

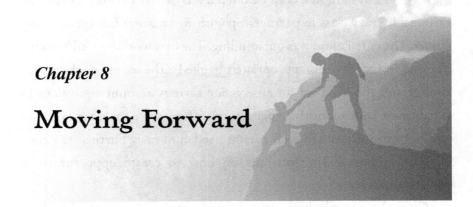

Chapter 8

Moving Forward

A S THE POTENTIAL IMPACT THAT opening earlier in the evening and having the security of being year-round could have, it was realized that we were in a unique position. Several clients were coming to the shelter by 5:30 PM. The need to be more intentional about our service offerings was recognized. After several weeks of research, the decision was made to open our transitional/supportive housing program. This program was uniquely designed and research based. The first identified need was the importance of case management.

A case manager is a cross between a coach and a social worker. The case manager is a motivator and cheerleader for the client who partners with him or her in setting goals, benchmarks, appointments and structure. The case manager holds the client accountable and helps the client move forward and accomplish his or her goals one step at a time.

The program was set up to provide extra support to clients who were ready to make meaningful change to their lives and their circumstances. This 120-day program addressed the systemic issues that lead to homelessness utilizing strategic means. Many of our partnerships were utilized to provide onsite classes that addressed the systemic issues which lead to homelessness.

In early 2014, the first class we offered was Secure Futures, a five-week financial literacy class in partnership with *Renaissance Entrepreneurship Center*. The curriculum was outstanding. The first week covered banking (the importance of being appropriately banked). The second week covered savings and the need for an emergency savings account equivalent to three times your monthly expenditures. There were in- class exercises to determine how much each person needed to save. Further, the class included brainstorming sessions on how to create opportunity to realistically save.

Class three taught budgeting. Each person made an actual budget. The purpose of this section was to free people from the fear of making a budget and the idea that a budget is a bunch of rules. The goal was to teach everyone to think about a budget as an opportunity to decide how each person wants to spend their money. Classes four and five were about credit and debt. It provided the necessary information to help our clients make informed choices.

The class was a tremendous success. The curriculum included positive peer pressure as well as weekly homework assignments. If at least 60% of the class completed the assignment, money would be included in a drawing on the last class. There was a potential to win up to $200. The students were excited and researched different banks and credit unions, created budgets and created savings plans. The atmosphere was filled with hope and positivity.

One lady who was in the class was in her 60's. She had been homeless for several months, but was new to our shelter. She had a retirement from her previous job of several years. She also had a part-time job. Although she had a long work history, she never had a savings account. The idea of saving money was a foreign concept to her. The class was very enlightening for her. An additional benefit for completing the class was the opportunity to receive a grant from the *Opportunity Fund*. This was a two for one matching grant over a one-year period. In other words, a client had the opportunity to save up to $500 over a period of 12 months by making monthly deposits of between $25 and $45 dollars. The rule was that each person was required to make a monthly deposit and not spend the money. After 12 months, the Opportunity Fund would match their savings up to $1,000. This client was the very first person to take advantage of this opportunity. She became excited each month as she saw her savings account grow. This motivated her to open an additional savings account and save as much money as she possibly could.

Not only that, but this fantastic program also provided a Secure Credit Card to those who chose to take advantage of this opportunity. She took advantage of this as well. By the time she left the shelter, she increased her credit score by over 100 points. Additionally, she had over $4000 to help her move into her new apartment. When following up with this client a few months ago she informed us that she now has over $10,000 in her savings account.

Another class that we could offer our clients was through Healthy Relationships California, a non-profit with a research based Problem Solving/Communications curriculum. A certified instructor taught this five-week onsite class once a week. Clients received needed tools to help them communicate more effectively and work through their disagreements by more constructive means. There were several success stories that were a direct result of this class. Clients were learning how to problem solve instead of yell at one another. Staff members heard many positive things from clients regarding this class and asked if they could take the class as well. We allowed it, as we realized that it provided additional training to our staff.

We continued to expand our courses and contracted with a local therapist, LaTonya Takla, to offer Life Skills and Anger Management. Clients were taking advantage of the onsite opportunities to receive assistance. Some of our clients had court ordered anger management. These classes qualified, as they met the requirements of the court. The staff were motivated. The clients were excited.

We added additional classes which included Art Therapy, taught by a licensed Art Therapist. This was a highly popular class. The clients expressed themselves through beautiful pieces of artwork which we eventually displayed. Momentum was building and we complimented our program by adding a 12-step recovery program, Steps to Betterment, a communication and problem solving class taught by a licensed therapist, as well as Anger Management. Everything appeared to be heading in a positive direction. We received multiple compliments regarding the quality of our programs from the community.

As in most circumstances when change is taking place, everyone was not on board. Unfortunately, some of the resistance came from some of the staff members who had been with the company for several years. They began to do things to undermine the organization and some of the employees. Additionally, they tried to divide the team. At first, some of their tactics were not recognized. These were seemingly good people. Many of the things that they did were background tactics. These tactics had profound impacts on the leadership team and the integrity of the entire organization.

Chapter 9

Positioned for Growth

W HEN SOMETHING GREAT IS BORN it needs to be positioned to grow. Growth is a natural part of life. Science shows us that if something is not growing, it is dying. Part of healthy growth is maturation. In other words, a healthy organization will learn from their mistakes and put systems and processes in place to strive towards success. This equates to change. We have all heard the statement, 'the definition of insanity is doing the same thing repeatedly and expecting different results.' This may sound very cliché, but it is true. With every obstacle, there is an opportunity to learn and grow. If an organization is not growing, those in charge need to take a closer look and see what is hindering the growth. It is not productive to continue down the same path when your organizational system has proven time and time again that it is not producing the needed results. Instead, it is essential for the leadership to assess what obstacles are stifling organizational growth.

There are several reasons why organizations do not grow, but the main causes can generally fit into three categories. The first is infrastructure. This deals with both the physical edifice as well as the internal organizational makeup. Sometimes the building is no longer appropriate to sustain growth. This could be due to the building size or location. It may be too small, not have a large enough parking lot, may not be practical for construction, be difficult to access, or a host of other possibilities. In a case like this, it may be better to sell (or rent) the property and purchase another building, or have a custom built building.

Regarding infrastructure as it pertains to the organizational makeup, sometimes the organization may need to add strategic positions, hire a consultant, update their strategic plan, develop an advisory board, or make a host of other operational adjustments. A common occurrence is when the board of the organization is no longer operating at its intended capacity. This is a touchy subject, as some organizations do not have term limits for boards. Avoiding term limits sets an organization up to maintain ineffective board members, thus resulting in stagnated growth and limited potential. Remember, there are the 4 G's of board members – give money, get money, give meaningful advice, or get off the board. It may sound harsh, but it is true. Board members can become 'drunk with power' and stifle the long-term growth of an organization. Additionally, they may suffer from burn out, yet refuse to retire. Those struggling with burn out become highly negative. This is very common in social service agencies and churches. They may even be struggling with compassion fatigue.

Further, it is imperative that organizations, churches, etc. have the right people on their team. This does not exclusively pertain to management, although the wrong management can cause things to go downhill rather quickly. This pertains to the entire staff. One practice that I learned early in my career is 'hire for personality; train for skills.' This is because you can have a highly skilled person on your team with a horrible personality. The work ethic or personality can become a schism in your organization. Often highly skilled people think of themselves more highly than they ought. I understand that it is not always possible to do this. Certain fields require specific skills. However, personality

---

should still be a key factor in the hiring decision process. Remember, you must work with this person daily. Also, this person is a representative of your organization.

It is often more effective to hire someone who is less skilled with a great personality. If the person is eager to learn you can develop him or her. This provides an opportunity to invest in someone who will stay with your organization for years. Project WeHOPE stands for We Help Other People Excel. We have found tremendous success in abiding by this principal. Additionally, it is important to match your employees with the mission and vision of your organization. This helps put everyone on the same page which results in less inter-office fighting, which can be a huge distraction. Everyone needs to have the same 'map' to effectively work together and accomplish a common goal.

The second obstacle that can hinder growth in an organization might be the processes that you have in place. This can also be described as bad management decisions. Pastor Bains often says, 'If it's not the people, it's the process. If it's not the process, it's the people.' Sometimes organizations have established processes that are not effective. They may have been effective in the past, but may no longer be relevant. It is paramount that organizations keep up with the times and the current best practices. This does not mean that they change their vision or mission, although it might mean that they need to be adjusted. It means that they keep abreast of the latest trends and assess if their business practices are relevant.

The third reason organizations do not grow is that they have the wrong people in the wrong positions. This can result in a negative environment. Everyone is not intended to be at the same company, church, etc. for their entire lifetime. However, owners, pastors, managers, tend to want to hold onto them. Some people are intended to be there in the beginning to help get the journey started. They may have a unique ability to encourage and support the mission at the initial stages of the venture. The problem comes when they are ready to move on and the organizations continues to hold onto them. Often managers will panic and offer the employee a raise to entice him or her to remain loyal to the company. Generally, when a person decides to leave, it is due to more than just financial reasons. If they stay, the same reasons that they wanted to leave are still there. They may stay temporarily, but it is generally not long term.

When someone communicates that they are ready to move on, don't try to change their mind. Listen to them and give them your blessing and a reference. Convincing them to stay is a mistake that will become an obstacle for growth in the future. Eventually the organization will realize that the person is no longer a good fit. Unfortunately, the owner, manager, pastor, etc., talked them into staying, so getting the person to leave will be extremely difficult because they have become a disgruntled loyalist. They will expect the organization to show them the same loyalty they showed the organization. This further perpetuates a negative environment.

Once an integral team member leaves, it is necessary to take the time and use the necessary resources to fill in the gap. This can become an obstacle. It is difficult to find the right fit for crucial positions in your organization. You may be tempted to quickly hire someone out of necessity. On one hand, this may seem like a promising idea, but on the other it can be disastrous. You must find someone who is able to help launch your organization forward and not simply fill a position. The person needs to have the right chemistry with the team. They need to understand, believe in and support the mission of your organization. To simply bring someone in to meet the company need can ruin your reputation. If you are in a situation where you are without an option, always, and I repeat ALWAYS bring that person in on an interim basis.

Keep in mind that each organization was birthed out of a vision to meet a need in a community. There are people who need what organizations or churches bring to the world. To go without it would create a void. Therefore, it is fundamental for an organization to be positioned for growth. The community is blessed by what organizations provide.

Chapter 10

Recognizing our Strengths

O NE OF THE MANY TALENTS of Project WeHOPE is recognizing a need and figuring out how to meet it. Several additions to our programs and services were direct results of this strength. For example, one of the administrators read an article that discussed shelter best practices. The article articulated how smoking among the homeless is prevalent and when homeless clients congregate and smoke in public, it reinforces negative attitudes amongst community members regarding homeless individuals. Therefore, best practices suggest that shelters have a designated smoking area that is out of the public view. After making this discovery, we realized that our smoking area was highly public. After some brainstorming, we decided to utilize a concrete slab located behind our shelter. This area was weatherized and modified to meet the need of our clients. This modification addressed additional safety concerns as well as provided a more comfortable environment for our clients.

Between five and ten percent of homeless adults have pets. Generally, the pets tend to be dogs and cats, but there are homeless individuals who have snakes and birds as pets, but these are few and far between. Most shelters do not allow pets due to allergies, fleas, and potential disturbances to the clients and the staff in the shelter. This becomes a barrier to people entering shelters. They want to make sure that their pets are safe. A young Girl Scout visited our shelter with her mother and asked why we didn't have a pet kennel. This was something that we wanted to have, but didn't have the time and resources to allow it to materialize. The Girl Scout was compelled to do something about it. She put together a fundraiser with her troop and the help of her mother. Within a few months she had a full plan and the funding to put her plan into action.

She returned to our shelter with her plan in place. She worked with *Menlo Church*, who was already scheduled to do a beautification project at Project WeHOPE. Together they built a pet kennel, ran pipes for plumbing, and purchased pet cages for safety. The finishing touch was adding the roof to the kennel. We were excited to be the first shelter in the County to have a pet kennel. It took a while for us to accept our first pet because we realized that we needed to have policies in place and provide proper training to our staff. Writing the policies was not difficult, but finding someone to provide the training proved to be challenging. It seemed like each place inquired about had road blocks. Eventually information was obtained from online resources so that the pet area could officially open. The first pet was accepted without incident.

Another need identified was birthed out of safety. Our clients were expected to be in the shelter by 7 PM. This was a recommendation of the County. The exception came if someone was working or had an obligation that they informed us about. Sometimes people would come into the shelter feeling hungry at various times. They did not have access to food that they wanted. Therefore, they wanted to walk to the store in the middle of the night to purchase food or a soft drink. This became an interesting topic of debate among staff because our clients were adults. Some of the staff members felt that denying the clients the right to shelter reentry for a snack run was cruel. Others were concerned that some of the clients would abuse drugs or alcohol and return to the shelter intoxicated or high.

The issue was discussed in a staff meeting and it was decided to purchase a vending machine. A vending machine would address the core concerns of the clients and the staff. Additionally, a vending machine would provide petty cash. This cash could assist clients with transportation and a host of other things that came up. The machine was purchased and stocked with many of the client's favorite snacks and beverages. We included a couple of heartier items for people who missed dinner. The clients were extremely excited to be able to purchase cold beverages and snacks onsite.

Upon further research on best practices in shelters, it was discovered that most transitional programs have a mandatory savings program for their clients. We recognized that most of our transitional clients were not saving money at all. This reminded me of a saying that my mother had when I was a child, 'Money burns a hole in the pocket.' In other words, many people feel the need to spend money immediately after they obtain it. The notion of saving money is a foreign concept. After doing additional research, our savings program was implemented which required clients to save a minimum of 30% of their income in a special account. Some clients were not thrilled at the idea of saving, but others were eager to save. After a brief period, most of our transitional/supportive housing clients were onboard.

A process to track each client's saving was developed and a system to hold him or her accountable. There are multiple testimonials that came from this program component. Several clients moved out of the shelter with enough money to be self-sufficient for a couple of months. Some clients purchased cars with their savings once they exited the shelter. Others had emergency situations arise and had money available to meet their urgent need without having to borrow from Check Cashing places or obtain predatory loans.

Our Financial Literacy Class reinforced our savings program. It also occurred to us that we were training our clients to pay their rent by requiring them to save a minimum of 30%. Financial counselors suggest that a person's rent or mortgage should be approximately 30% of their income. This practice helps people live within their means. The other added benefit is that it helped our clients maintain their housing by developing the habit of turning over a portion of his or her check.

The final need that will be mentioned that we recognized and we were able to meet was for our case management services. Most organizations desire to be highly competitive in their segment of the market. Project WeHOPE regularly looks at our successes and setbacks and poses the question, 'What can we do better?' This question often leads to brainstorming sessions which produces additional questions. One of the ways in which we wanted to grow was in our case management. The leadership wondered how we could improve our services and meet the needs of our clients more productively. Once again, Project WeHOPE researched accredited case management certification programs. After several weeks of research, a program was located that would not only meet our needs, but exceed the requirements of our civic partners. The admissions counselor was called and a deal was worked out that provided a discount for our case managers. Project WeHOPE would have the ability to enroll each case manager and send the payment.

The training was highly challenging. It pushed our case managers more than they had ever been pushed before. It covered medical case management, which provided a new perspective for Project WeHOPE. This additional training afforded us the opportunity to restructure this portion of our services to become more intentional and more housing focused. It also provided the opportunity for us to assure that all our case managers had the same training base, so that there was a more stable foundation to build upon.

Look at your company, church, non-profit, your life, etc. and ask the question, 'How can we improve?' No matter how good something is, there is always room for improvement. This is a part of the growth that was mentioned earlier. Remember, if something is not growing it is dying. This is Science 101. The more curious you become, the more open for growth you become.

Chapter 11

The Power of Forgiveness

A S PREVIOUSLY MENTIONED, THERE WERE several situations that occurred which resulted in disappointment, discouragement, and feelings of betrayal. Some of these incidents had the potential to destroy relationships permanently. Project WeHOPE is a small organization. As with many small organizations, there is a close- knit community and gossip spreads like wildfire. Unfortunately, when gossip starts, communication breaks down and damage control must be unleashed. What made our situation particularly unique was the fact that Project WeHOPE was started by a pastor. Pastor Bains was there onsite. The weekly messages that he preached at his church were on forgiveness and reconciliation. He provided several motivational teachings in our weekly staff meetings about peace, love and harmony. This provided an opportunity to demonstrate what was learned. There was a need to make a choice. It was pointed out that we could continue to wallow in what happened, after all, we could justify our anger and disappointment, or we could choose to forgive and move forward. Some of the team members elected to practice forgiveness and move forward. Others did not and are still harboring anger and resentment over things that happened years ago.

The decision to forgive is extremely difficult. It means letting go of all anger, animosity, and bitterness and the demand for justice in the situation. Human beings are wired for justice. It is unnatural to forgo this primal need. The purpose of forgiveness is more for the organization and the person forgiving than it is for the person receiving forgiveness. This is because holding on to anger and animosity is toxic. It destroys people and places. People who struggle with unforgiveness are bitter and angry people. Most of our jails and prisons are filled with people who are living with this incumbrance. It drives their decisions, keeps them up at night, and is the cause of much of the drug abuse and depression that encompasses their lives. Several studies have linked unforgiveness to disease (http://www.cnn.com/2011/HEALTH/08/17/bitter.resentful. ep/index.html?htp= c2

'Unforgiveness is like drinking poison and expecting someone else to die (Marianne Williamson).' It's best to let it go. Stop focusing on who got away with what and instead place your focus on strategic growth and lessons learned. The longer you delay the process, the more hindered your company is for augmentation. The very people wallowing in unforgiveness are the ones placing obstacles in the way of forward progress. Unforgiveness is like having a chain around your neck and living daily with that burden. I speak to clients in the shelter on a regular basis. Most, if not all, of them are struggling with unforgiveness. I have listened to their stories and they break my heart. I have had multiple discussions with clients regarding forgiveness because I have experienced the results in my personal life. No one is strong enough to carry the burden of resentment.

Unforgiveness affects places by changing the very atmosphere of an organization. It is as if a negative spirit enters the room and takes control of the moods and behaviors of the people. It creates a disdainful ambiance that permeates the actual environment and character of those caught in its web. Often the people who walk into the venomous environment plagued with unforgiveness will know that something is uncomfortable, but will not be able to pin point the source of the contaminate. They will dread being in the very presence of this atmospheric pandemic that is affecting the mood, tone, and feel of the room. This negative spirit can infiltrate businesses, churches, and well- meaning organizations. I implore you to get rid of this spirit immediately. It is destructive and all consuming. To eradicate this spirit, the people who feel as if they have been wronged must make the decision to forgive.

Many people struggle with unforgiveness because they have a misunderstanding of what forgiveness means. Let me clear up a few things about forgiveness by explaining what forgiveness is not. Forgiveness is not saying that what the other person did was okay or acceptable. Forgiveness is not letting a person get away with something deplorable. Forgiveness is not a coping mechanism to help you compartmentalize what happened. Forgiveness is not remaining cordial on the outside, while holding deep seeded resentment. Forgiveness is not pretending like the pain or the hurt is not there. Forgiveness is making the decision that despite what the person did or said, you have decided to release it and to release them of the penalty and some of the consequences for what happened. It's like giving someone a pardon from the Governor, but with results that penetrate the heart and mind of the person providing the forgiveness.

So, how does one forgive a person? To forgive a person, one must recognize that they are suffering and living a stifled life by carrying the burden of unforgiveness. They need to realize that they are doing a disservice to themselves and that practicing forgiveness is for their benefit. Additionally, they must release the person who hurt them from the debt that they feel the person owes them. That requires that they genuinely verbally say, 'I release (insert person's name) from all debt that I feel owed for (insert whatever they did). I consider their debt to be paid in full and they owe me nothing and I speak good things over their life. I hope they prosper. I hope they live a great life and find peace, fulfillment and happiness. When a person can say this from their heart, then they know that they have practiced authentic forgiveness. Sometimes thoughts will resurface and the person must remind themselves that this transgression has been forgiven. They must consciously make the decision to move on from that thought and focus on something constructive. This sets the person and the organization free to grow and prosper. It removes an enormous obstacle that could potentially become crippling and destructive.

An organization must realize that asking the people who have felt as if they have been wronged to forgive is an arduous task. Some people will get angry and become filled with self- righteousness. They will not take any responsibility for the part they played in the event. Things can become so tense that the environment initially becomes more hostile. Project WeHOPE experienced this. There were times that the staff meetings were so draining that people needed to take a break after a brief meeting just to detox from the negativity. There were times when it seemed as if things were improving, only for the rage and anger to increase in a couple of days. It was as if we took two steps forward and two steps back.

Some of the employees left the organization because they were highly stressed. This eased some of the tension, but until the majority of those who remained could exercise authentic forgiveness, things were still challenging. Fortunately, some members of the team attended a forgiveness seminar at Saint Samuel Church and others attended various trainings to help mitigate the forgiveness process. Throughout this trying time, we learned that not everyone would buy into the idea of moving forward. We continued to offer kindness and support to those who were still struggling until they reached a space where they were ready to move on from bitterness to healing.

Chapter 12

Additional Setbacks

PROJECT WEHOPE APPLIED FOR AND was awarded a grant (which was a forgivable loan) of nearly half a million dollars to aid in the purchase of our building. We had been leasing the building for 17 years. The owner of the building had decided to sell the building we were leasing as well as the building next to it. He is related to Pastor Bains so he was willing to give us a below market rate price. Purchasing the building was a strategic move which positioned us for further growth. We were extremely excited of the prospect of owning and we began to strategize about the diverse ways in which we could expand. We had a retired architect donate his time and one of our clients with this type of experience assisted in the preparation. Then we went as far as to hire an architect to finalize the new plans, begin discussions on the capital campaign, and have open dialogue about it in our staff meetings.

We went to the City to discuss next steps and immediately an obstacle was placed in our path. Although the property has multiple addresses and appeared to have distinct delineation, this was not the case. The property was classified as one parcel of land, so to purchase our building we needed to have the lot line adjusted. This was something out of our wheel house so we consulted with an engineer. The necessary paperwork was gathered to move this project forward. For two years we were stonewalled. Every time it looked as though we were moving forward, we were pushed back to the starting line. This was becoming increasingly frustrating. The building owner was losing patience, the organization providing the grant needed a completion date, and other local organizations wondered when this project was going to move forward.

It seemed as if this was an obstacle that could not be overcome. Then we started to brainstorm again. With that, it was decided that we had spent so much time trying to adjust the lot line, why not instead purchase both buildings? This seemed like the most logical solution. Therefore, the process began for the exploration of the possibility of owning both buildings. As this option was pursued, the City got involved and claimed that we were operating without the proper permit. Things reached a boiling point. Fortunately, a wonderful volunteer on our side went through the files and showed that we did in fact have the proper permit. The Planning Commission had made a mistake. Unfortunately, by the time that this mistake was discovered, there was a danger of losing the money that would be used as the initial down payment for the purchase of the building.

Fortunately, Pastor Bains went to the granting organization and received an extension. Everyone breathed a sigh of relief and then the next obstacle came out of nowhere. Several viable plans were in place to move forward with purchasing both buildings when the owner changed the purchase terms. The change that he made rendered it impossible for us to purchase both buildings. Everyone sat in disbelief for a couple of days. The leaders were devastated and wondered how this could be overcome. This last-minute change came seemingly out of nowhere. This was a very difficult position. There was already an extension from the granting organization. How on earth were we going to pull this off? We thought that we had a solution and it fell through. Now what?

I want to once again pause and state that even when you have brainstormed and found a solution which meets the core needs of all parties, there will still be obstacles and resistance. When you have put in numerous weeks, months, or possibly years of work and everything seemingly comes crashing down, you are sometimes left in a state of shock. For many, this shock becomes paralyzing. Many people become stuck right here. The disappointment can become the very obstacle which blocks you from ever completing your project. This is the place in which I refer to as being 'about to cross the finish line.' For some reason, we get the idea that when we get on this positive trajectory that everything is supposed to become smooth sailing. In a perfect world, this might be the case, however we live in an imperfect world.

This may become your biggest temptation to throw in the towel and not move forward. I say to you once again, DON'T QUIT! I know that it is difficult. I know that it is painful. I know that you are growing weary. I know that you have invested so much time, energy and resources. I realize that the money may be running out and you feel spent. Success is demanding work. It means each time you get knocked down (and you will) you must keep getting back up and becoming stronger and more determined than ever. Project WeHOPE experienced these frustrations. We did not move forward for several days due to the shock and disbelief that we felt. Once we allowed our wounds to heal, we continued to persevere.

The decision was made to reach out to a realtor to explore the possibility of purchasing a different building. According to the City, there was only one area with the proper zoning to open a shelter. There were a few buildings available for sale in that area. We decided to drive over and look at the buildings. They were much larger than what was currently used and much more expensive. The possibility wasn't ruled out, but the mere thought made us nervous.

At present we are going down parallel tracks. There is still work going on towards a subdivision so that the building that we are utilizing can be purchased. A lot of money has been put into this building by installing air conditioning, insulation, restrooms, a meeting space, etc. Additionally, a few local non-profit organizations invested in building modifications. We love our current building, but recognize that it is only a building. The vision is held in our hearts and if this means relocating, we are willing to make that sacrifice.

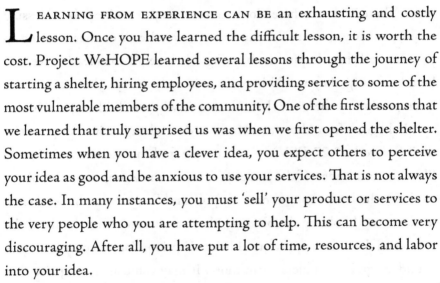

Chapter 13

Lessons Learned

L EARNING FROM EXPERIENCE CAN BE an exhausting and costly lesson. Once you have learned the difficult lesson, it is worth the cost. Project WeHOPE learned several lessons through the journey of starting a shelter, hiring employees, and providing service to some of the most vulnerable members of the community. One of the first lessons that we learned that truly surprised us was when we first opened the shelter. Sometimes when you have a clever idea, you expect others to perceive your idea as good and be anxious to use your services. That is not always the case. In many instances, you must 'sell' your product or services to the very people who you are attempting to help. This can become very discouraging. After all, you have put a lot of time, resources, and labor into your idea.

This is often another place when temptation to quit arises in your mind. When this temptation arises, don't quit. Persevere. Hang in there. Another thing that frequently happens when you find yourself in this space is that you take your focus from the vision and put it on yourself. You begin to complain about all the things that you have done and start to feel like you are not receiving the amount of respect or appreciation that you deserve. This is the moment when you need to talk to that good friend who will 'give it to you straight.' Stop listening to the people who are always on your side. Instead talk to the 'tough love person' who can help you get over yourself. Remember, He is the one who gave you the vision in the first place. He's got this!

As mentioned in chapter 7, Project WeHOPE began as an organization without paid staff. It was operated by volunteers. As more money began to trickle in, Pastor Bains wanted to provide stipends for the volunteers to show his appreciation. At the time he was volunteering and working 12 hours a day to keep this organization operating effectively. There were some people who were very excited to receive a stipend for work in which they previously volunteered. Others felt like they deserved more. There is a lesson here. Sometimes when you decide to be a blessing to people, they don't understand the personal cost of that blessing to you. Instead they despise the blessing. However, if the blessing were to be taken away, they would become extremely angry. This can present a temptation to the giver. I think that is why the Bible says, "Do not withhold good from those to whom it is due, when it is in your power to do it (Proverbs 3:27, ESV)." Some people find themselves in situations like this, as a leader. If the leader focuses on the wrong attitudes of the workers, the leader may choose to 'pull rank' and teach the workers a lesson by withholding the blessing; they can become angry and tell the person off. I would propose an additional option. You can pray for God's abundant grace and bless them more. It may come as no surprise that Pastor Bains sought to bless them more. Eventually Project WeHOPE was able to add salaries and benefits.

As mentioned in chapter 6, Pastor Paul and Cheryl Bains are pioneers. Some of the most extraordinary people are pioneers. Most people are not pioneers. Many people are settlers. These are the people who inhabit the land. This is also necessary. Most people are settlers. Settlers are followers. They do not tend to be people who take the lead. This is great because every leader needs some followers, otherwise the leader becomes a person who is simply 'going for a walk.' People sometimes use the term settler in a negative connotation, but it is not negative when used in this context. Everyone is not intended to be a leader. Yes, most people can be developed to take on leadership positions, but until the opportunity presents itself, it is better to be a settler or a leader in training. Imagine if everyone tried to be the leader. It would be chaos and mayhem. It would be an additional obstacle. Many organizations struggle with this issue and so did Project WeHOPE. A few people who worked for this organization wanted to be in control of things in which they were not assigned. They wanted the organization to run their way. This caused a distraction for a couple of months until Pastor Bains put his foot down and took control of the situation.

An organism with several heads is generally viewed as a monster. Monsters are frightening and unstable. It is not the way one wants their organization, church, etc. to be viewed or operated. It destroys the very core of the organizations functionality. This does not mean that an organization should run as a dictatorship, as this is also unhealthy. There should be oversight and processes in place to insure accountability because, 'absolute power corrupts absolutely (John Dalberg-Acton).' It is imperative that roles and responsibilities are clearly defined and that there is a governing board to oversee the final decision maker.

Another lesson we learned is that some people become insecure by other people's success, especially if they feel like someone may be passing them up. This can become a huge obstacle. If you find yourself in this circumstance, don't get discouraged, that person simply does not see the vision that you have, and that's okay. They never received the vision, so how can you expect them to see it? The answer on how to proceed in this type of situation can vary greatly depending on the circumstances. The first thing to consider is your personal stake in the company. How long have you been there? What is your position? What would the impact be if you were to leave?

Another consideration is the position of the person who does not see the vision. Are they the owner or an employee? If they are not the owner, is it possible to speak to their manager or the owner without causing too much friction? If the person has been there for a long time, are they nearing retirement? The answers to these questions can help you gain perspective and answer the question 'should I stay or should I go?'

As I started my new position at Project WeHOPE, there were a couple of employees who worked for the company who were less than thrilled about my new position.

'You know that the only reason that you were hired here is because I don't have the degrees that you have. If I did, this would be my job.' This is one of the first conversations that I had with one of the employees as I started my new job.

I was a little surprised by the boldness of this statement. It taught me a valuable lesson in humility. Fortunately, I responded professionally.

'I hear what you are saying. My position is interim. This means that I will only be here for a year or two. Perhaps when my assignment is over, this will be your job. I would love to work with you. We are a team and I have a lot to learn from you too.'

It is not unusual when a new person comes into a management position in an established company for people who have been working there longer to feel angry and resentful. In most cases, the person does not confront the new manager that directly. However, when this happens, it provides an opportunity to show the love of Christ through compassion and understanding. It also provides the opportunity to show professionalism. When these situations present themselves to us, we can allow ourselves to be offended and react to potentially offensive and inappropriate comments. What good will that do? Instead, we can choose to listen beyond the words that were spoken to the meaning of what was said. We can recognize the fear, hurt and disappointment and respond to that. This provides the opportunity to keep our character intact and build fundamental relationships.

Unfortunately, these fundamental relationships were not built and division began to set in. One of the ways in which the organization was becoming divided was by the disgruntled staff saying negative things about other staff members to service providers, community members and clients. On one occasion, a staff member approached me to discuss the staff rivalry. At this point I was not aware that there was a rivalry or that I was included in this rivalry. I was living with blinders on and occupied with organizational growth. As I paid closer attention to body language and comments made during staff meetings and by clients, I realized that there was divisiveness within the organization.

There is a lesson here. Sometimes management can be so focused on projects, growth, and development that they fail to notice things that are happening in their immediate surroundings. This can leave room for negativity to increase and for long-term damage to occur. Make sure that you pay attention to the important things, not just the urgent things. Regularly take the pulse of the environment and be aware of the things that are going on when you are not around. To neglect or ignore these things can mean destruction to your company, church, board, etc. Once you recognize what is going on, you cannot afford to wait or delay. It will get worst, not better if it is not handled immediately.

'The truth will make you free.' This biblical statement has been used in many different contexts. It is imperative for organizations to live in truth and not self-deception. Even if the truth is ugly, it is important to operate in it. You see, it is necessary to face the negative things that are going on within an organization. Once you face them, they can be mitigated. There is nothing more discouraging for employees to be a participant in the inauthentic reality that occurs when inauthenticity becomes the organizational culture. It can cause high turnover. Most of the clients, staff members, board members, etc. may be aware of the proverbial elephant in the room. When management does not address it, several different things can happen.

First, you foster an environment of dishonesty and pretense. When employees do not feel comfortable with managements relationship with the truth, they may gain the perception that management does not care or that management is disinterested. For those that are involved in the wrong doing, they may begin to feel that since management knows and is not doing anything about it, they are co-signing on the inappropriate behavior. This sends mixed messages to the entire team.

Another negative effect that may occur is that team members may lose respect for management. Perhaps prior to the incident, people felt confident in their managers. They may have felt safe and protected. When chaos begins to erupt and is not addressed, they begin to question the integrity of the entire organization and the managerial structure. Once this occurs, productive team members may decide to jump ship from a company they love and value. This can result in long-term ramifications to the company as well as to the individuals who departed.

Unfortunately, Project WeHOPE management did not respond quickly. Instead we tried team building activities instead of handling it head on. This caused a huge fall out for the company. It caused a great deal of long-term pain, damaged relationships, and thousands of dollars spent on counseling and intervention. In a previous chapter I referenced a scripture found in Mark 3:25 'A house divided against itself cannot stand.' This same statement was made by Abraham Lincoln during his speech on June 16, 1858. The statement was true then, and it is still true today. Maintain a healthy relationship with the truth. Then your organization will be free to make the necessary decisions to continue to grow and flourish.

It has been said that the wisest person learns from other people's mistakes. Every organization that has been in business over six months has a number of lessons they have learned. If you are just starting your business or church, you are strongly encouraged to talk with experienced organizations to help you avoid the mistakes that have been experienced by others.

Chapter 14

Dignity on Wheels

Dignity on Wheels 1

E VERY ONCE IN A WHILE, an idea will come to mind that can alter the entire course of your organization. It may be a new or innovative way to enhance the quality of your product or service. It may be an advancement in technology that enables you to do things much more efficiently than before. Whatever it is, these 'things' can be game-changing. For Project WeHOPE, our 'thing' was Dignity on Wheels. I want to take you back to August of 2005. A destructive storm hit the Gulf of Mexico. This storm became known as Hurricane Katrina. It was one of the costliest natural disasters in U.S. history and was a deadly monster that forever changed the state of Louisiana. A staggering 80% of New Orleans alone flooded, leaving waters that did not recede for several weeks. Nearly 2000 people were killed because of this catastrophic storm. The National Guard assisted with rescue efforts. Thousands sought refuge in the New Orleans Convention Center and the Superdome.

During this devastating time, Tide developed their 'Loads of Hope' program. This is a semi- automatic truck with a large bed specially outfitted with Whirlpool washers and dryers. This truck deployed to different areas to afford the people the opportunity to wash their clothes and provide hope and dignity during all the devastation which encompassed them. Pastor Bains saw this truck on television and was inspired. He thought about what a necessary service this truck provided and how he would like to be able to invent something like that one day.

Fast forward to 2013. Morris Chubb, Project WeHOPE board chairman had the idea to provide shower trucks in the community which could travel to encampments and other places where the homeless congregate. He brought this idea to Pastor Bains, who was already overwhelmed with the changes taking place with Project WeHOPE. He was surprised at how the idea matched thoughts of his own. He mentioned to Morris that it would be great to include not only showers, but washers, dryers and toilets. They were both excited and inspired. Pastor Bains told Morris, 'This is a pregnant idea and you should give birth.' In other words, he gave Morris the charge to get the ball rolling. A few weeks later, Morris came to Project WeHOPE with a medium size model with a truck and the custom trailer. He had this built to scale. Pastor Bains was shocked at how quickly Morris acted. He realized that Morris was very serious about this project. Morris had already researched companies who could build the trailer and had pricing established. Together they worked up a budget to 'give birth' to this idea.

Shortly thereafter, Pastor Bains met with Bill Somerville from Philanthropic Ventures, shared the vision and showed him the model. He was highly impressed and committed $45,000 to help this project come into fruition. Afterwards, First Congregational Church approached us and wanted to hold a fundraiser for Project WeHOPE. They raised thousands of dollars, so we were well on our way. As we continued to discuss this project and a potential timeline, Morris and Pastor Bains continued to share the vision with community members and organizations. People started reacting negatively to the concept. They felt that this type of project would enable the homeless to remain in their homeless condition. The support that seemingly came out of nowhere dissipated instantly. Morris began to feel discouraged. He was tempted to give up on the idea. Pastor Bains remained optimistic. He believed in the idea strongly and was not about to let a few naysayers influence this vision.

Several weeks later Pastor Bains and Morris went to a house party with some friends from a local church. There was a wealthy man there who had heard about their idea. They did not attend the meeting to discuss the project with him, however the opportunity presented itself. The gentleman liked the concept and wanted to help. They left the gathering excited that this kind gentleman understood and appreciated the concept. Shortly thereafter, they were contacted by this man and he informed them that he wanted to provide $200,000 to help move this project forward. Project WeHOPE now had the funding needed to have the truck built, retrofitted, and have the customized trailer assembled as well as 18 months of operating expenses.

I want to pause here and inform you that no matter how brilliant your idea is, there will always be the obstacle of naysayers. It is best to expect them so that you are not caught off guard. If you listen to your naysayers you will never accomplish anything. Think about it, there were people who told Michael Jordon that he would never play basketball. Steve Jobs received a lot of initial negative feedback when developing the computer. The Wright Brothers were told that the plane they were inventing would never fly. Henry Ford was told that the Model T car was a terrible idea. Why would you expect everyone to provide positive feedback on your vision? It's unrealistic. Sometime the naysayers will be friends, family members, potential donors, church members, board members, or even your spouse. If you have done the necessary research and have received some positive feedback through a needs assessment, keep pushing forward.

Word began to spread about this innovate way to reach the homeless. A writer for a magazine interviewed Pastor Bains and wrote a compelling article. Someone from Tide read the article and called us. They wanted to give us a year's supply of laundry detergent. Tide contacted Downy who also donated a year's supply of Downy. An executive from a local upscale hotel contacted us because they wanted to donate $10,000 of towels. We were surprised by the overwhelming support of major donors and large companies. Additionally, San Mateo and Santa Clara Counties each provided $50,000 grants towards this project.

Then the time arrived for us to build the truck. Everything happened much more quickly than anticipated. As a result, staff were both excited and nervous at the same time. Our design was in place and the money on hand, - now it was time to take a leap of faith and pursue the goal that had been set. The truck was to be built by the manufacturer with a flat bed so that it could be retrofitted with a six-hundred-gallon water tank and a generator. This meant that we would have to coordinate with two different companies for the truck as well as the company who would build the trailer. Pastor Bains and Morris took the lead on this.

There were multiple phone calls, emails, and discussions to help us assure that the timeline would work. The truck and trailer were built and assembled on the East Coast. Project WeHOPE is in California. Therefore, someone had to be sent to pick them up and drive them back once they were completed.

Fortunately, the timing worked out impeccably. Further, one of our Project WeHOPE partners, Pastor David Shearin, Lead Pastor and Executive Director of *Street Life Ministries*, was a former truck driver and was available to fly out and bring our vehicles to their destination. At first, things were going smoothly. Pastor David did a Vlog of the trip and we waited with anticipation to see the truck and trailer. Pastor Bains flew to meet Pastor David for the last leg of the drive. While they were driving the trailer started to detach from the truck. Due to the truck driving experience of both Pastor David and Pastor Bains, they recognized the problem immediately and were able to pull over and handle what could have been a catastrophe. Fortunately, this resulted in only a short delay and they still arrived in record time.

They arrived on a Sunday evening. Project WeHOPE staff toured the truck and trailer on Tuesday. It was so exciting to see this dream become a reality. Our marketing director contacted a company to design and create the decals for the unit. The company was remarkable. Everyone loved their designs. One was selected and the 'naked truck' was clothed in bubbles, our logo, and the names of the generous donors who helped make this program a reality. Once the truck was registered and ready to go we had our grand opening. We received an outpouring of support from County agencies, politicians, social service agencies, Whole Foods, and various other donors. Our launch was a tremendous success. Several homeless individuals showed up to witness history unfolding.

We hired a coordinator who worked diligently to connect with homeless service providers so that Dignity on Wheels would provide service where other social services had dissimilar services. Things got off to a great start. We received multiple emails and phone calls of congratulations. Many of the people who called wanted to know how they could partner with us and get involved.

A couple of months after our launch, Project WeHOPE hosted our annual breakfast fundraising event. A local gentleman with a family foundation attended the event and toured the truck. He wanted to help us extend our service area and funded a truck and trailer to help us accomplish this. The experience that we had already gained with our first unit motivated us to make a few adjustments on our second unit. For example, the first unit has two full restrooms consisting of a shower, sink, and toilet in each room. Additionally, it has two washers and two dryers. Experience taught us that fewer people needed to utilize the toilet. Therefore, the design of the second truck included only one toilet. That design modification afforded us the opportunity to add a third shower. An additional modification was that we added two additional dryers to better leverage our laundry services.

Our services expanded as we secured a contract with the City of San Jose. We doubled our capacity within months. This was exciting on one hand, yet nerve racking on the other. The excitement came because we could service more people in communities with limited housing resources available. The people whom we serviced were grateful to utilize our laundry and shower facilities. We were gaining more and more recognition. The stressful part of growth came with finding the right people to join our team. It is difficult to find people with the personality and temperament needed to operate on a site with partner agencies. This became an obstacle for us, so we reminded ourselves of what we learned in the past which was: hire for personality and train for skills.

Interestingly, in June of 2016 we received a phone call from a gentleman who heard about Dignity on Wheels and the idea motivated him to build his own trailer. He called to inquire if he could come to our site and see our design. We were glad to oblige. He came to the shelter and toured both of our units. Afterwards he came in and spoke with Pastor Bains. He decided to have a unit built in Los Angeles with a different design, but with similar functionality. He contracted with a company to have his trailer built not realizing how much of his time and energy would be required to see the program through to completion. He spent several months going back and forth with the builder until he became frustrated and no longer wanted to be directly involved with the project. He called and informed us that he did not have the energy or physical resources to continue. However, he wanted to assure that the trailer was built to provide services to the homeless. He wanted to donate the frame to us along with $40,000 to complete the job. We were informed that if we needed more funding to complete the trailer we could come back and request more.

This lead to the decision for us to acquire a third unit. Numerous phone calls and email inquiries were coming in, so we knew that the need was there. Pastor Bains and Cheryl traveled to Los Angeles to see the frame that had been built for the new trailer. It was vastly different than our design, so we brainstormed regarding how we could make it work. During this process, the builder wanted the trailer to be moved from his warehouse. Therefore, we sent a driver with one of our trucks to Los Angeles to pick it up and bring it to its new home. The local contractor that we are working with was not able to complete the trailer. We are currently raising the funds to have the third unit built and determine how the frame of the donated one can best be utilized to serve the homeless.

Dignity on Wheels provides more than showers, laundry, and restrooms. We have many success stories of how the lives of many of the people we serve have changed. For example, there is one gentleman whom I will call Steve. He started using Dignity on Wheels at our first site in Redwood City. Steve has a skin condition known as scabies. Once he started taking regular showers, it cleared up and went away.

There was another gentleman who was homeless and was scheduled to go on a job interview. He had not had the opportunity to have a shower and was concerned about how he would be perceived. The thought of attending the interview in an unclean state was intimidating to this gentleman and he contemplated not attending his interview. On the way to his interview he saw Dignity on Wheels at the social services agency and came and took a shower. This resulted in a change in attitude and motivation. He was now excited to go to his interview.

Not only that, there are several families in the community who live in their cars with their school age children. Often the families don't have the opportunity to bathe their children. Sadly, some of these children bathe less than once a week. The lack of clean clothing and a bath causes them to not want to attend school. Dignity on Wheels provides them the opportunity to give their children regular baths. Additionally, we connect the people we service to needed benefits which they are eligible for through case management. We have successfully housed approximately nine families and connected over 20 people to medical services. Further, we deployed to San Jose during the recent fires which rendered several families homeless. Dignity on Wheels truck and trailer provided on the spot service to the individuals and families in need.

As we have continued to grow and expand this program, Dignity on Wheels has received worldwide recognition. More specifically, we have been contacted by eight countries, been broadcast on KQED, I heart radio, a television station in Germany, and KLOVE radio. We have received requests from 27 states and 43 cities because people are impressed with what we have done. They ask if we will help them start and get a program like ours off the ground. Some want to know if we can come there and provide services to their communities. One of the most humbling events was being honored with the 13th Congressional District non-profit of the year award for 2016 by Senator Jerry Hill.

Our goal is to eventually launch Dignity on Wheels throughout several additional communities in the Bay Area as well as Los Angeles, who has an unprecedented number of homeless individuals. We would like to have our units in several other states around the country. We recognize that case management is one of the most essential components to aid in the success of this program. Case managers connect people to needed services and play an instrumental role in assisting them to become permanently housed, which is our primary goal.

Dignity on Wheels 2

Chapter 15

Continued Expansion

EXPANSION HAS CONTINUED TO BE a priority for Project WeHOPE. From the start of the organization, growth was the intended outcome. Pastor Bains and Cheryl had a vision for the East Palo Alto community. They desired to be change agents to a city plagued with violence, poverty and homelessness. After several successful operational years of the shelter, we desired to add a job training program. Through research and brainstorming we created HOPE Jobs, a program that would operate onsite and provide job training in the security field, custodial technician field, and food service industry. We selected these fields because there was not another local organization providing training in these fields, these fields are low barrier, so most of our clients would qualify, and the opportunity for clients to start their own businesses in these fields.

After identifying the fields in which we would train, we began to research organizations who we could partner with in order to bring training to our shelter. The first organization that seemed feasible was located all the way across the country. I went to their website and saw that they provide local training. I called and left a message. The representative returned my call the next morning. We had a wonderful conversation at which time, I shared the vision with him. As the conversation continued, he realized that one of their master trainers was located a few miles from Project WeHOPE. He put me in contact with the trainer. I called and invited him to the shelter to take a tour. After the tour, I brought him into Pastor Bains office and shared the vision with him. Then I explained to him that I wanted him to teach the custodial technician classes onsite.

Perry was used to teaching huge custodial classes and conducting seminars all over the country. This was a little outside of his element. He is an author of three books, has training videos online, and is highly experienced. He is a humble man and was moved by the vision. After thinking about what I suggested, he paused for a moment and then informed me that he would provide a proposal within a week. At the same time, I found out about a grant that was available for job training and creation. I applied for the grant and included my personal hope of what would be Perry's fees in the proposal, hoping that he had this same number in mind. When I received Perry's proposal, the amount that he proposed was the exact dollar amount that had been placed in the budget. I was so excited that I could barely contain myself. I felt as if it was a sign that HOPE Jobs was about to become a reality. Lo and behold I was right. The Foundation believed in our program and recognized our 17 year history. Therefore, we received the grant.

Things were going great, but they were about to get better. Perry has multiple connections in the custodial technician industry. When I mentioned that he was moved by the work that we are doing, it was not an exaggeration. He wrote letters to several companies and they sent several donations valued at thousands of dollars. For approximately a month, the shelter was inundated with boxes of supplies. It was like a long and exciting Christmas with endless gifts. Perry's kindness and generosity provided an opportunity for our clients and staff to be trained with state of the art equipment. Once again, our original expectations were exceeded.

Perry's slogan is, 'Working Smarter, not Harder.' He recognized that he needed to teach our staff to work smarter utilizing some of the top equipment in the industry. Not only that, but he helped us improve the shelter cleaning process and standards. Little did I know that one phone call would produce so many long- term results.

Each quarter, we have a graduation to honor our clients for completing classes. Some of our clients have never graduated from anything in their lives. Therefore, there is a ceremony with caps and gowns, medals, certificates, music, and a banquet. The clients march in to commencement music and there is a keynote address. Things are beautifully decorated because we want them to recognize the value of finishing what they started. The opportunity to invite their friends and family to attend is also provided. In this way the can celebrate the success of their loved ones. Prior to the first graduation that Perry attended, he reached out to the custodial technician training company and told them what we were doing. They were very excited about our partnership and sent one of the leaders from New York to attend our graduation ceremony. This kind man spoke during the ceremony and informed the clients that he had struggled with homelessness. His message was inspiring and encouraging and further cemented our relationship with this great company. Additionally, Perry addressed the attendees and stated, 'I teach classes all over the country, but this has been my favorite.' So many amazing things have been birthed out of this wonderful relationship. I continue to stand amazed on how it got started.

An additional component of our HOPE Jobs program is our security training. We contract with a retired security officer with over 30 years of experience. Additionally, we contracted with Mike, a local owner of a successful security business. He agreed to come to our shelter and issue the state certified examination as well as perform background checks and fingerprinting. This training program has been very successful because the security industry is in high demand. California requires security officers to have a guard card. It costs over $200 to go through the background checks and pay the fees to obtain a guard card. We offered the training and service to our clients and community through the grant that we were awarded.

Once we advertised these classes, security companies called and emailed Project WeHOPE offering to hire our graduates as soon as they obtained their card. This provided the opportunity to provide immediate job placement in addition to job training. Before long, people throughout the community were calling to take advantage of this opportunity. The demand was so high that we developed a waiting list. This program helped us to add a new dimension to the fulfillment of our vision. The impact was incredible. One of our staff members also graduated from this program and was able to obtain a part-time job to supplement her income. One of the clients in our shelter who had previously experienced difficulty obtaining work obtained his guard card. He was then able to find work right away and has been gainfully employed ever since.

This program has produced more success than we ever thought possible. Our goal for the future is to expand and grow this program to include both day and evening classes, as well as to eventually expand to other identified low-barrier high demand industries.

An additional need that we have identified is the need for medical respite dormitories specifically for the homeless. This need was identified because hospitals would release homeless clients to our shelter who need additional care. This is not a criticism of doctors or social workers. If the patients had houses to return to, they would have been perfectly fine. When a person is released to a homeless shelter there are specific variables which must be considered. For example, if the person needs bed rest, a shelter that is open for 16 hours a day is not the appropriate place to discharge the patient. Unfortunately, we kept receiving patients who needed additional assistance. The prohibitive cost of medical care is an issue that is discussed often in both political and social arenas. Hospitals routinely release patients more quickly than they did in the past. Further, it is best for a patient to heal at home rather than in the hospital amongst others with ailments. There were occasions when we had to return a patient to the hospital who had been released to us because it was not appropriate for the patient to stay at our facility. For example, if the patient was recovering from pneumonia, we could not ask him or her to be outside in the community. We could not morally do something that could cause harm to a person or set back his or her recovery. To mitigate this situation, we talked to local hospital administrators to assure that this did not continue to happen. It caused stress for the Project WeHOPE staff, administration, and to the patient.

One solution that we created was to utilize a space that we are renting to build a respite dormitory which would be staffed 24 hours a day with a nurse and an additional employee. This would meet the need of homeless individuals who needed bed rest to properly recover. It also would meet the need of local hospitals and enable them to release homeless patients in need of additional rest, wound care, breathing treatments, etc. It would also afford us the opportunity to better service the most vulnerable members of our community.

To meet this need the shelter leaders met with hospital administrators and local non-profits. An agreement was established with key stakeholders who were willing to help finance the on-going costs of the project once we could get it up and running. At the same time, a Request for Proposal was due for new construction projects which benefited the disenfranchised. I completed the request for proposal and the organization came for a site visit. They liked the concept and secured a construction company who would provide the modifications pro bono. We were highly excited. Another vision, another dream was about to move forward and assist those in need. Additionally, a volunteer architect offered to complete the drawings for us. This was gladly accepted and the drawings were made and presented to the City. The City required modifications. The architect made the modifications and the plans were resubmitted. Currently we are waiting on the approval by the City Planning Commission so that this process can begin.

People do not enter the social services industry to get rich. They do it because of the love they have for humanity. When you get to know people, who are struggling and suffering, there is a social justice cry that rises in your heart. It is heartbreaking to see people suffer. Someone once said to me, 'I bet that you are able to sleep well at night knowing the impact that you make in the lives of people.' For me, I feel blessed an honored to have the joy of participating and partnering with people to change their lives for the better. There are days and times when things are incredibly difficult, but the reward of seeing a client housed, a person who was too shy to talk in front of people, strut down the runway and model a new outfit at our spring Fashion Show Fundraiser brings us immense joy.

Life will always bring obstacles. Some of the obstacles are devastating and can be crippling if you allow them to be. Other obstacles can be seen more like road blocks. Regardless of what type of obstacle you encounter, know that every obstacle can be overcome. Sometimes it may mean severing ties with someone. Other times it may mean practicing authentic forgiveness. It may require gathering thought leaders together and conducting brainstorming sessions to develop creative ways to navigate through the situation.

I went through a difficult and painful experience at my last job. I worked with 2 amazing women. We had symbiotic relationships and things went smoothly for several years. A tragedy occurred which resulted in the reassignment of the team lead. The administration decided to replace the highly experienced team lead with someone outside of the department with limited experience. There was conflict from day one. I found myself struggling with job dissatisfaction for the first time in years. I reflected on my position and I recognized that I had encased myself in my own version of a glass ceiling. I realized that I was the only person who could control my destiny.

After much thought, reflection, meditation and good counsel, I decided to return to school and complete my master's degree. This ended up being one of the best decisions that I have ever made in my life. It elevated my thinking. Additionally, the advanced degree qualified me for several positions. This decision changed the entire course of my career. It put me on a trajectory that I never imagined possible. In other words, overcoming that obstacle changed my life for the better. Had it not been for that difficulty, I more than likely would not have returned to school and be where I am today. Overcoming hurdles helps you grow in ways that far exceed your expectations. Don't resent the obstacle; overcome it.

Project WeHOPE has experienced several obstacles. Through it all leadership and staff learned to trust our instincts, the pain of letting go, and the reward of moving forward. Our organization has experienced setbacks, yet we learned to overcome the obstacle of forging through a setback and finding victory on the other side. There is no special formula to overcoming. It takes optimism and determination to persevere no matter what comes your way. There will be frustration. There may be tears. There may be the temptation to quit. Don't quit! Muster up all the strength that you have and continue to forge ahead. If you fall, fall forward. At least then you will be headed in the continued direction of the success that awaits you.

Printed in the United States
By Bookmasters